MW00668891

IMAGES
*of America*

# THE FREE STATE OF WINSTON

**The Winston County Courthouse.** (Courtesy *Double Springs Scrapbook*, sketch by Tom Sangster.)

IMAGES
*of America*

# THE FREE STATE OF WINSTON

Dr. Don Dodd
and Dr. Amy Bartlett-Dodd

ISBN 978-1-5316-0381-6

Published by Arcadia Publishing
Charleston, South Carolina

Library of Congress Catalog Card Number: 00-104654

For all general information contact Arcadia Publishing at:
Telephone 843-853-2070
Fax 843-853-0044
E-Mail sales@arcadiapublishing.com
For customer service and orders:
Toll-Free 1-888-313-2665

Visit us on the Internet at www.arcadiapublishing.com

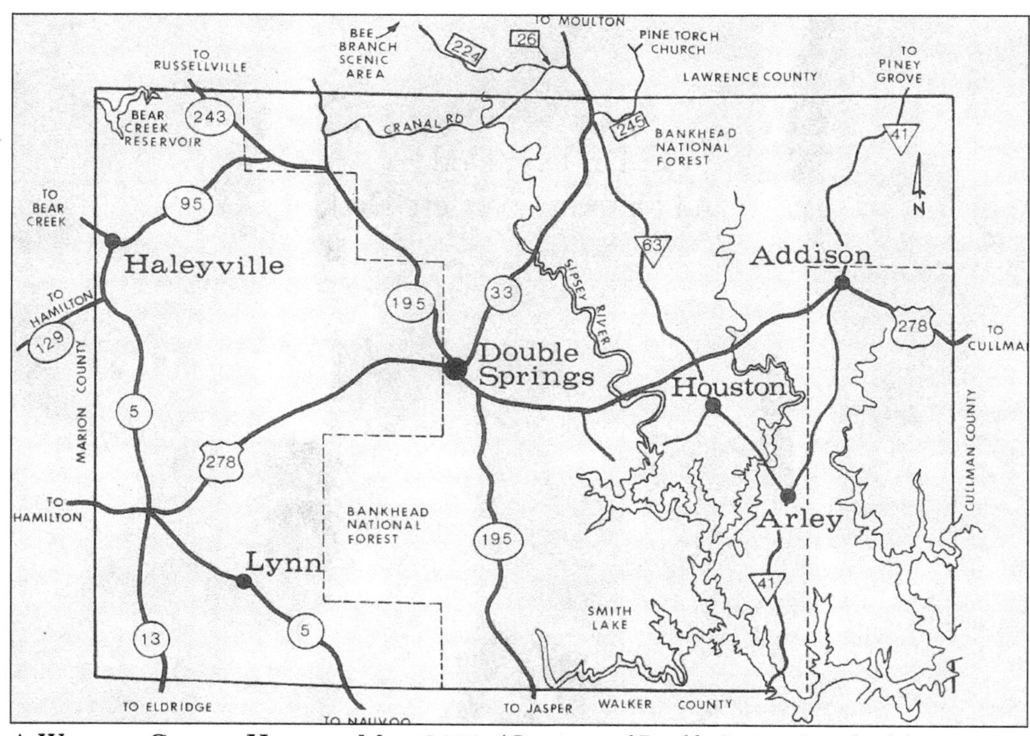


**A Winston County Highway Map, 2000.** (Courtesy of *Double Springs Scrapbook*.)

# Contents

# ACKNOWLEDGMENTS

It is with the greatest appreciation that we acknowledge the major sources of photographs that made *The Free State of Winston* possible. Members and friends of the Winston County Genealogical Society, through the help of Ronald and Darryal Jackson, contributed a large number of family photographs. Billie (Mrs. Ullman) Fortenberry generously shared her substantial holdings of Haleyville photographs and news clippings so numerous that her credit line, "Courtesy of Billie Fortenberry and the *Northwest Alabamian*," was abbreviated to "Courtesy of BF/NWA." Hundreds of photographs and sketches were collected through the years as the authors worked on other local projects.

Every photograph used has a credit line acknowledging the source of the image. A special effort to contribute a number of photographs, sketches, and/or information was made by the following: Doris Bartlett, the Birmingham Public Library, Jean Blanton, Gus Buttram, Sallie Cox, Yvonne Crumpler, Denise Pratt Cutcher, Eldon Curtis, Brad Dodd, Kinneth Dodd, Gerry and Melissa Rose Farris, Ullman Fortenberry, Donna Wilson Gunnin, Edward Herring, Carolyn Hunter, Ruth Johnson, Looney's Tavern Productions, Lamar Marshall, Beth McCandless, Donald McVay, Stella Woodard Pratt, Reba Feltman Riddle, Dess and Tom Sangster, O'Neal Shipman, R.L. Shirley, Loree Speer, Pat Taylor, Bill Tidwell, the U.S. Forest Service, Bettye Steele Watters, Cora Lee Peak Whatley, Maxine Wolfe White, and Doris and Hoyett Wolfe. Additionally, we pulled from the sources of the late Wynelle Shaddix Dodd and Myrtle Blake Lester. We regret being unable to use all of the photographs submitted. Often there was not sufficient information available to identify individuals or places in photos or images were too poor to reproduce well. Sometimes there simply wasn't an appropriate place or enough space to include a photo. We appreciate and value all of those submitted. It would have been a far more difficult job to create this book had there not been such a substantial number of photographs from which to choose.

Information for the captions came from a variety of sources. Most often those contributing photographs had critical and interesting information about the people or scenes depicted. Other sources included the Winston County Genealogical Society's *The Heritage of Winston County, Alabama* (1998); Dodd's *Winston: An Antebellum and Civil War History of a Hill County of North Alabama* (1972), especially for the Hancock County's 1850 Census, Winston County's 1860 Census, and the Cemetery Records of Winston County (pp. 165–203), which were alphabetically arranged and not in the index; Jerry Burns' *The History of the Clear Creek Baptist Association* (1957); Billie Fortenberry; and *The Northwest Alabamian* newspaper of Haleyville.

*The Free State of Winston* is the authors' second book with Arcadia. *Deep South Aviation* (historic photos from Birmingham's Southern Museum of Flight) was the first. Our editor for both books was Katie White, who was patient and encouraging while providing excellent editorial and promotional assistance. The entire Arcadia staff worked quickly and efficiently in processing the manuscripts to books ready for marketing. They do an exceptional job of preserving and documenting thousands of historic photographs that would otherwise be lost or unidentifiable.

It has been fun and satisfying to work with all of these individuals and organizations to produce a book that makes us proud.

# Introduction

Winston County was one of the last frontiers in the settlement of Alabama. Carved from northern Walker County in 1850, it was named Hancock County after the famous signer of the Declaration of Independence and nine-time governor of Massachusetts, then renamed Winston in 1858 for the first native-born governor of Alabama, John Anthony Winston. On February 12, 2000, Winston County celebrated its 150th Anniversary (1850–2000).

Geographically a part of the Cumberland Plateau, the southwestern-most extension of the Southern Appalachians, Winston was a hilly county with thin and infertile soils and thus was sparsely settled and economically poor—the poorest county in the state by the 1850 and 1860 censuses. Like the other hill counties of north Alabama, it was initially a land of small, isolated, 40-acre, one-horse farms and one-room log cabins. By the Graduation Land Act of 1854, land on the market for 30 years was reduced in price to 12¢ an acre, creating an 1850s land boom. Most settlers could only buy 40 acres ($5 worth), the smallest parcel available from the Huntsville Land Office.

To more affluent plantation owners in the rich-soiled Tennessee Valley and Black Belt, the hill country of north Alabama was just a geographic barrier to overcome. In fact, Alabama's first state road was the Byler Road crossing the mountains to link the Tennessee River with the Black Warrior River at Tuscaloosa (and from the Warrior River on to the Tombigbee River and Mobile). The recent Tennessee-Tombigbee Canal finally completed this link to empty the products of the hinterland of the Tennessee River Valley and more into the port of Mobile.

In the antebellum era, the hill country was missing two significant items—cotton and slaves. Hancock/Winston had the fewest slaves in the state in 1850 and 1860 with 62 and 122. Ninety-eight percent of the Winstonians of 1860 did not own a single slave. Winston ranked last (#52) in cotton production with 352 bales. The "Cotton Kingdom" did not extend into the hills of Winston.

Without cotton and slaves, Winstonians did not see the election of Lincoln in 1860 as a threat to their well-being or a valid reason for secession. They opposed secession in 1861 and sought to be neutral in the war that followed. When they held the famous Looney's Tavern neutrality meeting in the spring of 1862 and voted to be neutral, Confederate sympathizer Uncle Dick Payne remarked: "Oh, oh, Winston secedes! The Free State of Winston." Winston did not secede, but did ultimately furnish more troops for the Union Army than the Confederate and "The Free State of Winston" tag has stuck to the present.

Perhaps the "Free State's" reluctance to leave the Union during the Civil War was a part of a longer-range conservative resistance to change. In comparison to the mainstream South, the hill country has been the slowest to make major cultural changes from the 1850s to the 1950s. Winston County, due to geographic, political, and economic isolation, in many ways has been a stranded frontier for a full century.

Growing up in the late 1940s on a 15-acre farm at Poplar Springs (adjoining Bankhead Forest), Don walked to a two-room school that didn't have running water and had coal-burning stoves for heat. His family had a milk cow, hogs, chickens, one mule for plowing, fruit trees, truck crops for canning foods for the winter months, a smokehouse, a corn crib, Bankhead Forest for hunting, and Clear Creek for fishing and swimming. They didn't raise cotton and the family farmed what cultivated land they had without outside help. They had a hog killing in the fall, the first watermelon by July 4, fresh greens when it was too cold for anything else, and canned peas and green beans all the time. Don killed his first squirrel and caught his first fish at age nine. They cooked and ate both. Grandma Weaver lived with them after Grandpa died and she made lye soap in a large black pot over an outside fire. They took baths in a #10 wash tub with heated water from the same pot. How different was this from small farm living in the 1850s?

*The Free State of Winston: The 150th Anniversary* is a story of a mid-19th- to mid-20th-century north Alabama hill county cultural evolution. Underneath the available fragmented photos and descriptive captions is a continual, slowly changing society that produced values some of us old-timers think worth preserving. When Hoyett Wolfe says "we didn't make a living, we lived on what we made," it captures something for us. Spending an evening singing gospel songs with Wallace and Rose Ann Tidwell and listening to them sing ones we have never heard is a special memory. An afternoon reading Jerry Burn's *History of the Clear Creek Baptist Association* or the pamphlets of George Gibson of Arley are nostalgic moments. Hopefully this pictorial history will collectively convey similar images. Clark Woodard's family photos of split white oak basket-making, boat making, and bee-hive robbing likewise conjure thoughts of days gone by. Some of these cultural gems touch on universal themes of self-sufficient farm folks worldwide.

By looking into the photographs of 20th-century town life, the automobile revolution, consolidated schools, hotels, hospitals, and the rudiments of modern living, folks can see a remembered past. Through the study of local events we can observe history happening. Our folks fought wars, raised families, built homes, farmed, logged, ran stores, preached, taught school, and "lived on what we made." Winston County old-timers were rough-hewed, solid, durable folks like the homes they built—good ancestors with strong, time-proven values that can help us survive in a complex, modern world. The impact of this legacy is strengthened by our stopping short of recent times. So, except for a few preservation developments such as Bankhead Forest's Wilderness area and folks working to extend it and, of course, Looney's Tavern, we did not include the last quarter century. Read, enjoy, reflect upon, and preserve the legacy.

*One*

# Twentieth-Century Hill Country Living

**The James Peak Men Ready to Work in the Fields at Their Pleasant Hill Farm.** Pictured above are Jim Peak and sons Henry, Clifford, Virgil, Grady, Clyde, Howard, and friends of the boys, Ray Jones and Bill Little. Jim and his wife, Minnie Benson Peak, later moved to the Rock Creek community. (Courtesy of Cora Lee Peak Whatley.)

**The Hunter Family at Work, early 1900s.** The John Marion Hunter family readies for their daily chores in the Enmanfield community north of Addison. (Courtesy of Carolyn Sartin Hunter.)

**The Hunter Family at Their Home in Enmanfield.** John Marion Hunter, his wife, Martha Catherine Dyer Hunter, and their seven children lived in the Looney's Tavern Post Office District. Son Ollie served three terms as sheriff and son Bert taught school for 40 years, including service as principal of Double Springs Elementary. Sons Bert and Herb married Curtis sisters, Lucy Jane and Annie Mae. (Courtesy of Carolyn Sartin Hunter.)

**Baptizing at the Ward-Pickard Mill in the early 1900s.** "Dunk" Pickard's Mill, near Ark, was a favorite baptizing place of Tom Sutherland (1863–1938), pastor of the First Baptist Church of Haleyville from 1904 to 1905. First Alabama Cavalry veteran Anderson Ward had a mill here before Pickard. Jerry Burns, in *History of the Clear Creek Baptist Association, 1874–1957*, said Tom P. Sutherland "very probably baptized more people than any other man in this association in his most active years." (Courtesy of *NWA*.)

**Curtis Bluff School at Houston, 1905.** Miss Addie Blackwell (standing on the left, braced on a sapling) taught students under Curtis Bluff at Houston while the school was being built. Students and visitors are as follows, from left to right: (front row) Bill Speer, Enna Speer, Berta River, Cora Blake, Lee Blake, Mary Ballentine, Rossie Everett, Bertha Everett, Edgar Lee, Theodore Tidwell, Porter Rivers, Dick Speer, and Harry Speer; (second row, seated) Pearl Speer, Mary Speer, Dewey Everett, Carol Lee, Pinkney Tidwell, George Rowe, and Irma Ballentine; (third row, standing) Miss Blackwell, Pearl Rowe, Era Tidwell, Pearl Burdick, Edna Burdick, Dena Gregory, Agnes Rivers, Elsie Lee, Lillie Burdick, Erien Rowe, Icie Rowe, and Bertie Rivers; (fourth row) Dora Burdick, Mozelle Ballentine, Ira Speer, Zena Gregory, Mattie Hancy, and Minnie Gregory; (back row) Frank Gregory Stewart Ballentine, Jack Blake, and Cora Blake. (Courtesy of Myrtle Blake Lester.)

**The Speer Family Farm near Cornith.** Lenabell, Tommy, Sam, Jack, and Dora Speer are pictured at their homeplace. Note the two yoked oxen. (Courtesy of Loree Speer.)

**Robbing the Bee Hives at the Clark Woodard Farm.** Fletcher Robertson and his son Marcene fiddle while Fletcher's son-in-law, Clark Woodard (far right), takes honey out of a bee hive. The two children watching rather close to the action are Lucy (far left) and Valice (middle foreground). Their log house is in the upper left. (Courtesy of Stella Woodard Pratt.)

**Lee F. Dodd and Walter L. Shaddix Bicycling in Double Springs, 1909.** Lee and Walter take a break in front of the Tennessee Valley Bank, which served Double Springs until 1935. Lee's son, Lee Pershing "Pert" Dodd, married Walter's daughter Wynelle. Their only son, Lee, who piloted a terrain-hugging F-111 Aardvark in Vietnam, is now at the famous Lockhead Skunk Works in Palmdale, CA. Pert and Wynelle also had twin daughters, Linda and Susan. (Courtesy of R.L. Shirley.)

**Barnett School, 1908–1909.** Barnett School was built in the 1880s and named for Joe Barnett, who donated land for the school. Barnett consolidated with Calloway and Moreland in 1927 and all went to Moreland. In 1932, a Freewill Baptist church was organized in the building and it is now known as the Barnett Chapel Church. Alfa Hill (Wolfe) and her sisters, Berta and Allie, are in the photo. (Courtesy of Hoyett Wolfe.)

**Blue Springs School, 1909.** Blue Springs School was located 4 miles north of Double Springs off current Highway 195. Teacher Fletcher Corbin's students included members of the Godsey, Jackson, Lyle, and Martin families. Clarence Lyle taught here in 1921 at a reported salary of $64 per year. The school year was normally about three months between planting and harvesting. (Courtesy of Winston County Genealogical Society [WCGS].)

**A SUNDAY AFTERNOON OUTING, HALEYVILLE, 1913.** Haleyville folks gather at a bluff (perhaps at the Mineral Springs). They are, from left to right, as follows: (front) Coil and Maggie Bates Lindsey, Charley and Nettie Bates Miller, and W.E. and Lillie Bates Cook; (back) Irene and Noley Kilpatrick, Ollie Mae and Albert Cook, and Heddy Bates and Arthur Cook. (Courtesy of BF/*NWA*.)

**OLD HOUSTON SCHOOL (1913).** Posing from left to right are as follows: (front row): James Rowe, Cortez Burdick, Floyd Everett, David Blake, Virgil Blake, George Rowe, Burnett Ballentine, Theodore Tidwell, Roy Tidwell, Kelly Tidwell, Blake Rowe, Pernie Rivers, Grady Andrews, and Frank Hunter; (second row) Susie Waid, Lucy Waid, Ora Andrews, Pearl Speer, Emma Speer, Cora Blake, Agnes Rivers, Rossie Everett, Margie Tidwell, Erin Rowe, Nora Battles, Honor Tidwell, Mae Tidwell, and Alice Rivers; (third row) Dora Baird, Mary Ballentine, Pearl Rowe, Pearl Andrews, Era Tidwell, Irma Ballentine, Bertha Everett, Birdie Rivers, Bertha Rivers, and Lois Tidwell; (back row) Milner Hunter, Lee Blake, Porter Rivers, Pinkney Tidwell, Grant Burdick, teacher Young Blake, Willie Baird, Hilliard Waid, Mary Speer, and Loutita Andrews. (Courtesy of Alford Owen and *NWA*.)

**Drawing Water at Helican, 1919.** Jefferson (Jeffie) Chapell Woodard is shown drawing water the old fashion way. The well is still open today. Jeffie's husband was Berry Newton "Bud" Woodard (1864–1932), the son of Jesse and Elizabeth Kilgore Woodard. (Courtesy of Stella Woodard Pratt.)

**Hog Killing Time at the Woodard's.** From left to right, Clark Woodard, F.V. Robertson, and the youngster, Relton Robertson, share November slaughtering duties. Ham, shoulders, and middling were put in salt to cure. Liver, tenderloin, backbone, and ribs were fresh meat to be eaten in short order. Scrap lean meat was ground into sausage, fat meat cooked into "cracklins," and lard was saved for cooking. (Courtesy of Stella Woodard Pratt.)

**Robertson's Log Cabin.** Five people lived in this one-room log house—Fletcher and Susanna Wolfe Robertson and their children, Bellvene, Marcene, and Almon. Bellvene married World War I veteran Clark Woodard in 1919. Their first home in Helican was blown away by a tornado in 1920. (Courtesy of Stella Woodard Pratt.)

**Plowing and Sowing at David McCullar's.** The McCullar family plows a cornfield in preparation for planting at their farm south of Double Springs. Ronnie Jackson surmises they are sowing oats. (Courtesy of Jean Blanton.)

**A Curtis Family Syrup-Making.** From left to right, Daton Curtis, Lee Curtis (Mrs. Milford Curtis, daughter of Marion Williams), and Maudie Curtis watch the boiling as syrup is made. (Courtesy of Eldon Curtis.)

**Clark Woodard of Arley, 1923.** Having survived a 1920 tornado, by 1923 Clark and Bellvena owned an 80-acre Arley farm they bought for $400. They had four children: Anna (b. 1920) married Phyllip Hall in 1948; Newton (b. 1922) married Mavis Wilkins in 1939; Stella (b. 1927) married Cecil Pratt in 1949; and Aster (b. 1930) married Clifford Mattox. (Courtesy of Ken Pratt.)

**POSSUM HUNTING.** The successful hunters pictured here are Dewey Shipman, standing in the tree, and Riley Shipman, on the ground with the prey by the tail. (Courtesy of Neal Shipman, nephew of the possum hunters.)

**A 1940S FOX HUNTERS' CONVENTION.** Gathered in Winston County are quite a number of fox-hunting men and dogs. George Steele and Will Blankenship attended this convention. "Tittle's" was written on the back of the photo . . . perhaps referring to the Tittle community west of Lynn. (Courtesy of Bettye Steele Watters.)

**STEELE FAMILY BOATING, 1934.** Enjoying a boat outing on the Sipsey River are the following, from left to right: (front) Edna, Bettye (the baby), and Mavis Steele; (back) Mae Curtis Steele; Dennis, Loree, and A.B. Steele; Kit Steele Cole; George Newman; Lois James; and the dog, Bess. (Courtesy of Bettye Steele Watters.)

**MID-1930S CORNFIELD FUN.** Idell Frazier (Mrs. Ben) Little and I.V. Steele (Mrs. Luman) Cole harvest a bushel full . . . the diminutive Estelle Frazier (Mrs. J.J.) Bartlett. (Courtesy of Jerry and Jill Bartlett.)

**Center Dale School, 1926–1927.** The Cooper, Hill, Lane, Rowe, Speer, and Ward children attended Center Dale School near Corinth. (Courtesy of the WCGS.)

**The Smith School House Church.** This 1930s log structure was built in the Smith School House community to serve as a church and meetinghouse. It had 12 corners representing the 12 apostles. Both the community and church were named for the Smith School House at Arley built in 1911–1912. In 1923 it consolidated with Union Grove, Pine Ridge, Old Arley, Nathan, Bethel, Anton, Flat Rock, and Dismal to form Meek School. (Courtesy of Denise Pratt Cutcher.)

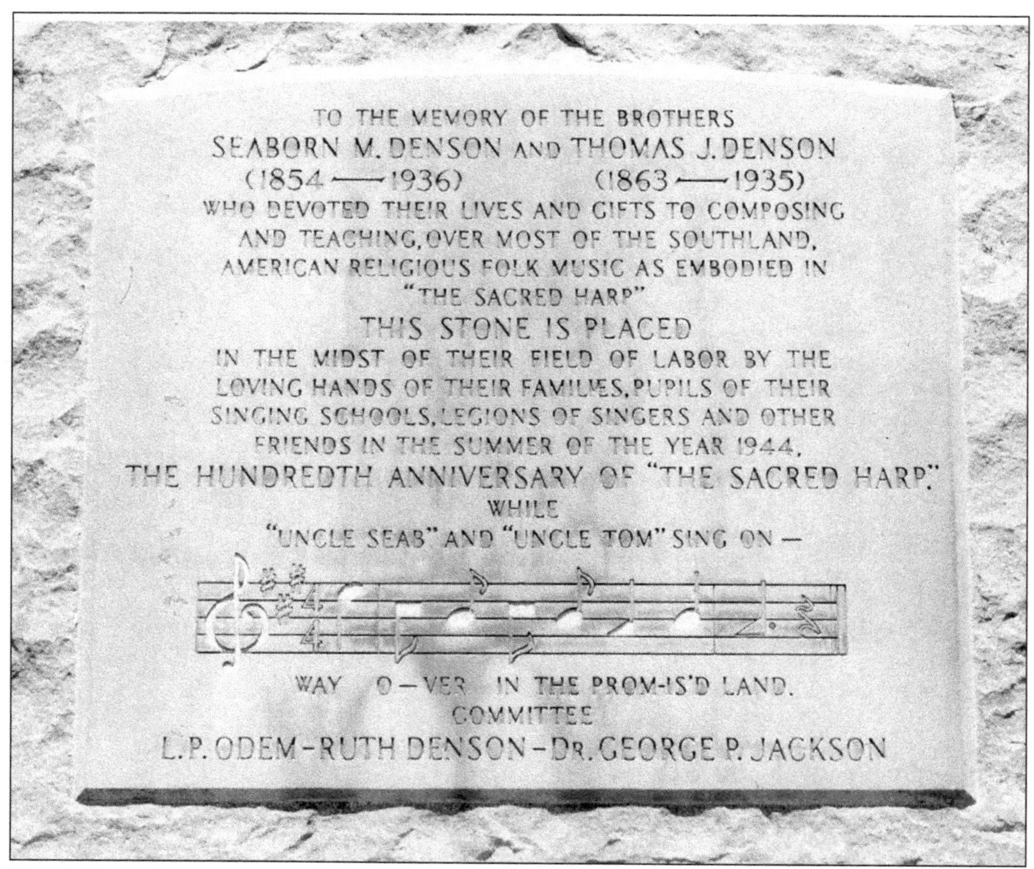


**The 100th Anniversary of *The Sacred Harp*.** Dedicated on the 100th anniversary of the publication of the original *Sacred Harp* song book, this monument was placed on the Winston County Courthouse lawn in 1944, honoring the work of two brothers from east Winston County. Seaborn Denson (1854–1936) and Thomas J. Denson (1863–1935) were famous "Fa-So-La" religious folk musicians, teachers, and composers. Professor George Pullen Jackson of Vanderbuilt University, the recognized authority on Southern Appalachian spirituals, made the principal address. Kathryn Tucker (Windham) of the *Birmingham News* recorded the story that "If a Denson child can't sing by the time he's three or four, the family drowns him." John Posey Sr., Judge John Bennett Weaver, and Judge R.L. Dollar were on the program. Dr. Jackson noted, "The Densons' greatest life achievement is seen today in the fact that wherever one finds a Sacred Harp one finds most of the singers have been taught by one or both of these brothers." (Courtesy of Amy Bartlett-Dodd.)

**Rock Creek Singing School.** Attending a singing school at Old Rock Creek Baptist Church in Double Springs are the following, from left to right: (front row): Ollie Hess, Izora Hess, Oma Dill Gardner, and Virgil Martin; (second row) Lillian Martin, Malcolm Martin, Jasper Martin, Wandell Hicks, Betty Snoddy, Wayne Cagle, Rebecca Haney, Betty Lou Hicks, James Martin, and Gladys Hicks; (third row) unknown, Preston Martin, Betha Martin, Jewell Hicks, Ina Martin, Ruby Steele, Boots Snoddy, Averit Haney, James Young, and Faye Snoddy; (fourth row) Viola Moody, Dee Young, Magene Cole, O.C. Snoddy, Kenneth Martin, and Pernie Martin; (fifth row) Mavis Steele, Edna Steele, Helen Steele, Rex Haney, Lois Hicks, Madeline Martin, Edward Hicks, Rufus Pool, Ed Snoddy, and Leldon Cole; (back row) J.T. Reeves, Jim Matt Curtis, Roe Hood, Tom Moles, and James Hood. The remainder are unknown. (Courtesy of Helen Steele Shipman.)

**The Williams Family at Hickory Grove Church of the Nazarene.** Pictured is the family of James Marion Williams. From left to right are as follows: (front row): Lee (Curtis), Jocie (Abner), Fairrie (Walker), J.M., Allie, and Dora (Connell), and Ada (Shirley); (back row) Henderson, Earnest, Oliver, Burville, Homer, Viola (Bailey), and Clara (Gibson). The girl in the middle is Martha Ann. (Courtesy of Eldon Curtis.)

**GARDENING.** Willie Mae Riddle works in her garden in 1988 at age 90. Born in Douglasville, GA, during the Spanish-American War (1898), she died in 1999 in the Grayson community at age 101. The daughter of Edgar and Ora Strawn, Willie Mae married Calvin Riddle and lived in one of the four houses Calvin made from a CCC camp barracks. (Courtesy of Reba Riddle.)

# *Two*

# Buggies, Trains, and Horseless Carriages

**Addison Women Go Buggying, 1915–1920 Era.** Traveling in the popular mode of transportation in their day are, from left to right, Azallie Cordellia Hunter (Mrs. Luther) Glover, Bertha Phillips, Annie Curtis (Mrs. Herb) Hunter, and Pearl Phillips. (Courtesy of Carloyn Sartin Hunter.)

**Some Had a Buggy.** Jim (1883–1958) and Laura Dunn and child take a ride in their horse and buggy. Jim and Laura had four children: Floyd, Wiley, Reba, and Theo. (Courtesy of Stella Woodard Pratt.)

**Mule and Wagon Days, 1924.** Clark and Bellvena Woodard, with their children, Anna and Newton, are pictured at Arley with their only transportation, a mule and wagon. (Courtesy of Stella Woodard Pratt.)

**The Lynn Depot, 1890s.** The building of the Northern Alabama Railroad through the Lynn area in the 1890s began the development of Lynn as a community. A temporary box car depot gave way to the Lynn Depot shown here. One-room log schools were consolidated into a three-room school at Lynn with three teachers by 1926; three more rooms added by 1929, and a new brick high school was built in 1935. By the 1920s, Red Bailey's planer, Charlie Long's cotton gin, and Albert Baughn's store were operating. Lee Dodd, Dave Long, Charlie Barton, and Bill Barton soon had stores. In 1931 two long-time Lynn institutions began—John T. Harris' store and Benny Barton's barber shop. A row of businesses and the depot emerged on one side of the tracks with the Lynn school complex on the other. (Courtesy of Kin Dodd.)

**A Painting of the Haleyville Depot, c. 1907, by Virginia Burleson.** Illinois Central (IC) served Haleyville from 1907 to 1988. As the crew-change point between Birmingham and Jackson, TN, most employees lived here. There was a mechanical shop and "round house" to service steam engines. Before diesel engines arrived in 1954, putting many machinists and road crews out of work, Haleyville was a major IC railroad town. (Courtesy of Virginia Burleson through Billie Fortenberry.)

**A Steam Engine Crosses the Quarter-mile-long Brushy Creek Trestle, the Longest Railroad Trestle East of the Rockies.** The trestle was built in 1907 with 1,209 cross ties and 36,000 pounds of rails. One worker was killed building the trestle and another while painting it in 1939. Nearby is the "Rube Burrow Cave," where the legendary outlaw supposedly hid after robbing the train, which slowed to a trestle speed of 20 mph. (Courtesy of Ullman Fortenberry and NWA.)

**The Illinois Central Railroad Turntable at South Haleyville.** The turntable turned cars and locomotives. When first installed in 1907, it was turned by hand or a team of mules. Later air hoses connected the locomotive with an air engine in the small house (above). About 400 engines a month passed through the shop. It closed in 1954 when the diesels came. (Courtesy of Ullman Fortenberry and *NWA*.)

**Illinois Central Engineer Warner M. Flack and His Son, John M. Flack, at the Haleyville Railroad Yard in 1925.** IC was a major contributor to the Haleyville economy and railroad work paid well. W.M. Flack owned the large house that was sold to the Snoddy brothers in 1928 and used as Haleyville's first hospital. (Courtesy of Dr. Betty Drake, granddaughter of Mr. Flack, through BF/*NWA*.)

**Illinois Central Rebuilds a Steam Locomotive Engine in South Haleyville.** At 120,000 miles or so, engines were stripped and rebuilt at a cost of about $10,000. The rebuilders are, from left to right, T.E. Knight, J.R. Knight, R.W. Parker, H.T. Fortenberry, J.B. Bates, R.F. Harp, A.F. Hulsey, H.C. Martin, A. Hyde, C.E. Miller, O.M. Finley, T.W. Cleveland, Lowell Kennedy, D.M. Crosby, G.E. Sisson, and J.T. Sisson, shop manager. (Courtesy of Billie Fortenberry.)

**Haleyville Prior to Urban Renewal.** Shown is Virginia Burleson's painting of Haleyville in the pre-1954 days when her husband, Ed, was engineer on an Illinois Central steam locomotive, like the one on the left. Haleyville was a railroad town, the yearly lighting of the Christmas tree was a major event, and urban renewal was far in the future. (Courtesy of Virginia Burleson through Billie Fortenberry.)

**The 1910-1920 Era in Double Springs.** F.O. Burdick drives past his home at Double Springs. He moved his family from Houston about 1910 so his children could attend the new Winston County High School (WCHS). His daughter Kate was a math teacher at WCHS for many years. Viola, another daughter, was also a teacher and married John Hosmer Campbell, principal of the new WCHS that opened in 1926. (Courtesy of Carolyn Burdick Hunsaker through Sallie Cox.)

**A Moreland Couple Buys a Ford in Haleyville, mid-1920s.** Mollie and Dewey Cochran (son of John Cochran) are pictured at their home with a new Ford from the Cowart Motor Company of Haleyville. On the wheel cover it is noted that "Another New Ford" goes "65 miles per hour." (Courtesy of Donna Wilson Gunnin.)

**MARCENE'S NEW 1927 FORD.** Marcene Robetson sits in his new Ford. J.B. Robertson recalls that Marcene gave $400 for it from Meron Rowe Fletcher, sitting on the running board, and Susanna Robertson (far right). A "Rev. Rowe" is on the left. (Courtesy of J.B. Robertson.)

**ANOTHER FORD, MID-1930S.** Melvin Poe stands by his car, perhaps a 1934 Ford. (Courtesy of Anna Woodard Hall.)

**COUNTRY DOCTORS MADE HOUSE CALLS.** James Samuel "Sam" Snoddy, pictured with his wife, Frances, in the 1920s, practiced medicine in Addison, Russelville, and Haleyville. He married Frances Kilpatrick in 1924. She died in 1929 and their son, Robert Samuel, was killed in World War II. Dr. Snoddy married Jane Prideaux Lakeman in 1933. Their two children, Bill and Galoria, graduated from Haleyville High and the University of Alabama. (Courtesy of C. Hiller Jr.)

**SMALLTOWN GROCERY STORES ALSO MADE HOUSE CALLS (DELIVERIES) IN THE 1920S–1930S.** In 1932, Sallie P. West wrote in the *Advertiser Journal* what one could buy for $1. At L.C. Fuller's one could get a "sack of good flour, two pounds coffee, and five pounds sugar." (Courtesy of Luther Tittle through *NWA*.)

**George Steele in an Early 1930s Truck.** George Newton Steele (1898–1974), son of Sylvester J. A. Steele and Sarah Elizabeth Taylor, married Mae Curtis (1902–1947) in 1917 and they had 11 children. George farmed, ran gristmills, grocery stores, service stations, and restaurants, and did carpentry and masonry work in the Double Springs-Haleyville area before moving to Florida in 1950. He died there in 1974. (Courtesy of Bettye Steele Watters.)

**A Speer Family Jeep Outing, 1948.** Don, B.C., and Loree Speer cross the Bull Branch bridge in their Jeep in this 1948 photo. About 12 years later, the bridge was removed. (Courtesy of Loree Speer.)

**The Speer Family Takes Their Show on the Road.** Mary Jane Estes Seymore Speer (1878–1949) and James Jackson Speer (1862–1933) of Houston pose in front of one of the cars that carried them to the gospel singing performances for which the "Singing Speer Family" was well known. (Courtesy of Donna Wilson Gunnin.)

**J.J. Bartlett, Double Springs Businessman, with His First Delivery Truck.** J.J. and Estelle (Frazier) Bartlett opened their first business in February of 1946. For 30 years they sold furniture and appliances including Norge (shown advertised here on the truck), Admiral, and General Electric. Retiring from the furniture business in 1976, Bartlett continued with Double Springs Motors, which he operates 54 years after going into business for the first time. (Courtesy of J.J. Bartlett.)

**Ben G. Dodd, Getting Ready to "Run a Route" for the Dodd Sales Company, Littleville, 1957–1958.** "Uncle Ben" (1892–1962) was a small businessman, Baptist minister, and Republican politician in Winston and Walker Counties for a half-century. "Bent over" from a coal mining accident, he used his handicap to good advantage in business, politics, and everyday life. He had a flair for the colorful, a comical wit, and the ability to entertain. (Courtesy of Don Dodd.)

# *Three*

# Gristmills, Sawmills, and Cotton Gins

**The Upper Falls of Clear Creek near Falls City.** A longtime water-powered gristmill site, the falls are now under the waters of Smith Lake. Painted above by Jean Cook, they have a colorful history. Oral traditions include a large Native-American camp and burial ground; a Native-American legend in an epic poem; its 1812 "discovery" by Jesse Livingston; counterfeiters in 1822; Benjamin Boteler's mill site in 1850; Wilson's Raiders in 1865; and Dr. Snow's Hospital in the early 1900s. (Courtesy of Don Dodd.)

**The Upper and Lower Falls of Clear Creek Falls.** Water-powered gristmills were the initial industries and Jess Livington's mill at the Upper Falls was probably the county's first. The Upper Falls fell 38 feet and the Lower Falls 42 feet. The pool below the Lower Falls was more than 75 feet deep. As Smith Lake is now 20 feet above the Upper Falls, the water depth below the Lower Falls is approximately 175 feet. (Courtesy of Wynelle Shaddix Dodd.)

**Kinlock Falls on Hubbard Creek in Bankhead National Forest and Hubbard's Mill Site.** David Hubbard (1794–1874), a Virginian wounded in the Battle of New Orleans, moved to the Tennessee Valley after the War of 1812. He promoted the first railroad in Alabama, was a member of the U.S. and Confederate Congresses, and had a summer home, "Kinlock"—the namesake for the falls, community, and CCC camp whose headquarters was in his summer home. (Courtesy of "Pert" and Wynelle Shaddix Dodd.)

**The Old Kelly Mill near Motes.** Kelly's Mill on Clear Creek was near the Cheatham Road crossing south of Motes (site of Godfrey College, 1880–1893). Barney Kelly ran the post office there and operated his gristmill. Barney was the great-grandfather of Jack Kelly of Haleyville, owner of the Cleere Hotel in 1949. (Courtesy of *Haleyville Advertiser*.)

**Winston County's Cash Crop.** Deputy Lee Moody (far left) poses with a confiscated whisky still in the 1920s. With no paved roads in the county prior to 1940, getting goods to market was difficult. Reducing weights helped transporting wagons over hilly roads with steep grades. By converting bushels of corn into a few liquid gallons, the hill people had a transportable cash crop, perhaps the major one. (Courtesy of Ronald Moody.)

**A Boiler for a Gin and Sawmill Arrives in Double Springs, c. 1909.** Andy Robinson and Lee Dodd ride two of the eight-mule teams used to pull the heavy-duty wagon (called a durgen) needed to transport a new boiler. Jeff Robinson stands between them. Among the others in the photo are Judge John S. Curtis, Dr. Tom Blake, Arch Brewer, John Garrison, Joe Howard, Sam Snoddy, and Sherman Walker. (Courtesy of Elmo Brewer.)

**The 1913 Multi-purpose Mill on Clear Creek West of Double Springs.** Sam Weaver Sr., Daniel Weaver, and J.C. Short built a dam on Clear Creek with a turbine wheel that served as a cotton gin, cotton press, sawmill, and gristmill. From left to right, Sylvester Stephens and six-year-old Jesse Davis sit in the wagon. Leroy Davis and Sam Weaver Sr. stand in the doorways. Others standing between them include William Davis, Graves Davis, Jim Short, and George Davis. (Courtesy of Jess Davis through the WCGS.)

**Hilton's Combined Sawmill and Cotton Gin in Double Springs, 1927.** The outline of Winston County High School, built in 1908, can be seen in the upper right. (Courtesy of Frank Wilson through the WCGS.)

**Big Logs Needed Hauling, Too.** One log, one wagon, two mules, and standing room only riders . . . now that's a log! (Courtesy of Eldon Curtis.)

**AN AERIAL VIEW OF THE HALEYVILLE TEXTILE MILL, HALEYVILLE'S FIRST MAJOR INDUSTRY.** The initial Haleyville Cotton Mill opened at this site in November of 1928. The industry was located in Haleyville due to the amply supply of electricity provided by the large primary substation built there by the Alabama Power Company in 1925 and the the IC Railroad, which transported cotton in from the Tennessee Valley. In the 1930s the mill paid a minimum of 30¢ per hour; this increased to 35¢ by 1941, at which time the mill employed 276. The above aerial shot is of the Kayser Roth Textiles plant in South Haleyville, which opened in 1951 and closed in 1987. In 1989 it was operated as Bama Textile. (Courtesy of Elmer Shipman through BF/NWA.)

**MACK WOLFE'S DAM ON SIPSEY RIVER, 1930–1940.** The concrete bridge on Highway 278 over Sipsey River replaced a steel bridge there in 1930. Mack Wolfe took the large rocks from the piers of the steel bridge and built a dam. Three small turbines in the east part of the dam powered a saw- and gristmill. Valice Robertson and his niece, Anna Woodard, are shown here posing at the dam. (Courtesy of Maxine Wolfe White.)

**A FULL VIEW OF WOLFE'S DAM.** Wolfe's dam, finished in 1940, was partially torn out in the 1960s to lower the water for constructing the bridge over Smith Lake. When the lake was completed, the turbines in the old dam were about 50 feet under water. In its 20-year history, the dam was a place of recreation for area residents—fishing, walking the rocks below the dam, wading, and swimming. (Courtesy of Hoyett Wolfe and Maxine Wolfe White.)

**Burdick's Gin, Addison, c. 1930s.** Burton and Fred Burdick's cotton gin in the center of Addison operated until decreased cotton production caused the gin to close in 1969. In its final days, the gin produced some of the cleanest cotton in the state because Winston's rugged hills did not lend itself to cotton-picking machines and most Winston cotton was hand picked. Burton graduated from WCHS at age 14 and the University of Alabama in 1926. He married Sarah Carrie Hester (1901–1983), an Auburn graduate and Double Springs teacher, in 1930. Fred was the Chairman of the Winston County Board of Revenue when he died in 1966 and was succeeded by his wife, Lura Williams Burdick, who died in 1970. Their only daughter, Freda, married Elmo Robinson Jr., the current mayor of Double Springs. Burdick-West Hospital in Haleyville was named for Fred and Talmadge West. (Courtesy of Don Dodd and Tom Sangster, *Alabama Hill Sketches*.)

**Wagons of Cotton Wait at the Haleyville Gin in the 1920s.** In 1930, the *Advertiser-Journal* estimated that 40% of Haleyville's income came from cotton, 40% from railroad and industry, 10% from crossties and lumber, and 10% from chickens, eggs, and produce. (Courtesy of the U.S. Forest Service.)

**The Arley Heading Mill, 1937–1949.** The J.R. Raible Company Heading Mill was Arley's first manufacturing plant. It built heads for slack kegs and barrels used to store or ship non-liquids such as nails and bolts. More than 100 new jobs were created by the mill, including some for women, especially during World War II. The mill closed in 1949 when labor negotiations could not be resolved. (Courtesy of Celia Sampley.)

**The First Chicken Broiler House in Winston County, 1951.** County agent W.L. Richardson laughs with R.O. Cleghorn of Arley, owner of the first broiler house in Winston County, in March 1951. Broiler production became a major industry in the 1950s and 1960s. (Courtesy of the Cleghorn family.)

**"Winston Uniform," Double Springs Industry, 1963.** Cora Lee Peak (Mrs. Frank) Whatley and Edna (Mrs. Paul) Bartlett make the first shirts in the new garment factory. W.T. "Bud" Eley, a native Canadian, brought his Michigan manufacturing business to Double Springs, providing sewing jobs for many local women. Changing over the years, it is known today as the "Double Springs Corporation," and continues to provide many jobs in the area. (Courtesy of Cora Whatley.)

# *Four*

# KINFOLKS AND FAMILIES

GEORGE WASHINGTON "WASH" (1874–1942) AND THE JANE (COWART) BLAKE FAMILY AT THEIR LOG CABIN HOME NEAR HOUSTON, C. 1890. Shown here are as follows, from left to right: (front row) Lee Blake, Jane (holding baby Virgil), Davis, and Cora Blake; (back row) Jane's parents, Thomas Jefferson and Lydia Ann (Chasteen) Cowart, standing next to "Wash" Blake (wearing a hat). Two other children, Myrtle and Lois, were born after this photo was taken. (Courtesy of Myrtle Blake Lester.)

**Cochran of Moreland.** Plez Monroe Cockran (1874–1905) was born in Paulding County, GA. He married Mollie Webb and they had six children: Meiford, Uyles, Lvey Cochran (Sewell), Hoston, Annie Cochran (Walker), and Ida Cochran (Armstrong). Plez and his wife are buried at Moreland. (Courtesy of Donna Wilson Gunnin.)

**William "Bucky"(1818–1900) and Rosa (1819–1908) Davis, Haleyville Pioneers.** Bucky entered 40 acres in Section 31 (now downtown Haleyville) in 1883 and built a log cabin on the Byler Road. The place became known as Davis Crossing and remained so until Bucky allegedly accepted a suit of clothes from the Haley brothers to affect a change. The *Haleyville Enterprise*, 1903, and *The Square Deal*, 1906, both recorded the new name as Haleysville with a "s." (Courtesy of BF/NWA.)

**The Robert Alexander Hill Family.** The children of Robert Alexander and Sarah Margaret (Lane) Hill are as follows, from left to right: (front row) William (Bill), John, Henry, and Robert L.; (back row) George Ann and Catherine N. Docia. This photo was probably made at Robert's house in Lynn (see p. 62). (Courtesy of Sallie Cox.)

**The F.O. and Catherine (Hill) Burdick Family, early 1900s.** Frank Oscar (F.O.) and Catherine are pictured at their home in Houston, near the Burdick Cemetery. Their children, from left to right, are Bob, Viola, Bernard, Kate, and Blaine. (Courtesy of Carolyn Burdick Hunsaker through Sallie Cox.)

**The Zadoc and Anna Lee McVay Family of Double Springs, c. 1911.** Pictured in front of their parents are Hugh and John, while Martha Ella stands in the back. Zadoc's father, John Anderson McVay, owned a farm at Brushy Creek. Zadoc attended Pine Torch School, Millport Farmers College, and Florence Normal. While serving as circuit clerk and later superintendent of education, he studied law. Zadoc subsequently served as deputy solicitor and tax adjuster. (Courtesy of Donald Morgan McVay.)

**The John and Nancy Elizabeth (Ingle) Dodd Family of Haleyville, c. 1896.** John Dodd (1844–1928), the son of Mikel and Mary "Polly" (Wright) Dodd, married the daughter of Andrew Jackson Ingle in 1868. The pair had 12 children. Four, Andrew M., Jessie, Nancy Jane, and Anna, died before this photo was made. The other eight and their parents are pictured above, from left to right, as follows: (front row) Otho, John (seated), Emma, Alta, and Mary; (back row) Mary Elizabeth, Rufus, Genia , Jasper, and Virgil Marion. (Courtesy of Rufus Sparks through BF/NWA.)

**The Wilson's of Houston.** Thomas David Wilson (1853–1937) and wife, Margaret Frances Hogg Wilson (1849–1924), of the Houston community, were the parents of George, Lucious, Sarah Lou, William M., Lavonia Ann, Samuel, Mary Emma, John Benjamin, Lee David, and Alberta Francis Wilson. (Courtesy of Donna Wilson Gunnin.)

**The William Wilson Family.** The William Mortimore Wilson family of Houston are, from left to right, Samuel Ralph (1904–1980), William (1876–1943), Claudia Faye Wilson Speer (1903–1986), Margaret "Maggie" Zerelda Tidwell Wilson (1883–1968), and Willie Mae Wilson Speer (1906–1992). (Courtesy of Donna Wilson Gunnin.)

**Willis and Belle Zena Farris of Lynn.** Shown are Willis David Farris (grandson of Sheriff Willis Farris), Belle Zena (Tittle) Farris, and their son Fred (the grandfather of Gerry, Terry, Kenny, Randy, and Kirby Farris). (Courtesy of Gerry and Melissa Rose Farris.)

**Mrs. Issac Tittle of Haleyville, 1922.** The mother of Luther Tittle and grandmother of Laura Tittle (Mrs. Ed) Laseter, sits near the Byler Road, later Twentieth Street. Across the street is the Summit Tidwell house (where Filo Howell lived) and to the right is Odie Dodd's house. The front of Dave Tidwell's store to the extreme right was later the newspaper office of the Haleyville *Spotlight*. (Courtesy of Luther Tittle through BF/*NWA*.)

**The F.O. Burdick Family in Double Springs, 1928.** The sons and daughters of Frank Oscar (F.O.) and Catherine (Hill) Burdick are pictured above. From left to right are Burton, Isadore (I.B.), Blaine, Robert, F.O. (father), Bernard, Fred, Kate (Hilton), Catherine (mother), Viola (Campbell), Harold, and granddaughter Catherine Campbell. All nine children graduated from WCHS and attended college—Harold to Auburn and the others to Alabama or Chattanooga. Most entered public service. (Courtesy of Sallie Cox.)

**The Dr. W.E. Howell Family of Haleyville.** Shown above are Dr. and Mrs. W.E. Howell and daughters at their home on Twentieth Street. Dr. Howell and his wife, Nancy, are seated. Their daughters are as follows, from left to right: (front row) Beatrice (Jackson) and Willie (Cleere); (back row) Leola (Miller), Julia (Drake), and Earlene (Foster). (Courtesy of Marguerite Wilborn through BF/NWA.)

**The Durald Curtis "Curt" Dodd (1863–1957) Family Reunion at Lynn, 1946.** Gathered for a family photograph are the following, from left to right: (front row) Gaylon Dodd, Billy Joe Dodd, Robert Dodd, Carolyn Dodd, Judy Holt, and Sandra Wakefield; (second row) James Earl Wakefield, Tommie Lou Dodd, Sonny Wakefield, unknown, Donna Lou Epperson (baby held by Martha Dodd), and Billy Gene Ellis; (third row, sitting) Durald Curtis Dodd and Martha Ann Manasco Dodd; (fourth row) Buddy Matthews, Don Holt, Bobbie Burns, Cecelia Dodd, and Martha Dodd; (fifth row) Dolly Matthews, Theodore Dodd, Olla Wakefield, Mary Maud Tingle Dodd, unknown, Buddy Burns, Jeanette Dodd, Tingle Dodd Epperson, Mack Epperson, Lanta Baird, and Nora Holt; (sixth row) Lucille Dodd, Nettie Lynn Dodd, Tom Dodd, Lee Franklin Dodd, Albon Holt, Audrus Dodd, Bill Dodd, Leon Dodd, and Willie Dodd; (back row) Earnest Wakefield, Durald Frank Dodd, and Charlie Holt. (Courtesy of Kin Dodd.)

**The Bartlett Family of Double Springs, 1951.** J.J. and Estelle (Frazier) Bartlett are shown with their five children. From left to right in front of their parents are Jerry (president, Athens State University), Jim (retired teacher), Tom (technical coordinator for the Winston County Board of Education), Amy (Jane) Bartlett-Dodd (former teacher, artist, and writer), and Ann Bartlett Preuitt (owner of Preuitt's Furniture Village in Hartselle with husband, Ken, of Addison). (Courtesy of J.J. Bartlett.)

**Steele Family Children Ride a Little Red Wagon.** This little red wagon, as noted on the side, came from Travis Crittenden's store in Double Springs—a large brick furniture store north of Dr. Malcolm Blake's office. From left to right are Mae Curtis Steele, Dois, Cindy, and Bettye Steele. (Courtesy of Bettye Steele Watters.)

**ULLMAN AND BILLIE (COOK) FORTENBERRY OF HALEYVILLE.** Ullman piloted a B-17 Flying Fortress in World War II and was a locomotive engineer for Illinois Central before and after the war. Billie, Haleyville's foremost historian, is the most knowledgeable person on the historic files of the *NWA*, based on years of research. She was the major researcher for the newspaper's centennial issue in 1989. (Courtesy of Ullman and Billie Fortenberry.)

**ALISON MCCREARY; MISS ALABAMA, 1996, THIRD RUNNER-UP, MISS AMERICA.** Alison, the daughter of Marc and Donna (Fortenberry) McCreary, is the granddaughter of Ullman and Billie Fortenberry of Haleyville. She attended Samford University, majoring in human development and family studies. Her volunteer work in the Brookwood Hospice program sparked her interest in helping children with the loss of a loved one. (Courtesy of Ullman and Billie Fortenberry.)

# *Five*

# Famous Folks and Houses

**Stanley and Lily Phillips' Home in Double Springs.** On the porch with the Phillips' is Lily's mother, Lucinda. Three of their children are Janie Frances, Willie Lou, and Stanley Oscar. (Courtesy of Joy Hampton McEwen.)

**Charles Christopher Sheats (1839–1904).** Sheats was a school teacher, delegate to the Secession Convention in 1861, unconditional Unionist, Union soldier recruiter, Confederate political prisoner, KKK target, congressman, and consul to Denmark. On his tombstone in McKendree Cemetery, near Hartselle, are these final words: "I love my country, my God, and my kind. I have served them all. I want no praise of song or prose." (Courtesy of Wynelle Shaddix Dodd.)

**Andrew Jackson Ingle (1820–1896), Founder of Double Springs.** Ingle was the leader in moving the county seat to Double Springs in 1883–1884. When the town was laid out, he built his home there. Ingle also built a portion of the sandstone courthouse in 1894. He and his wife, Rebecca Tittle Ingle, had nine children: Nancy (who married John Dodd), Kizzie (George Beard), Many (George O'Mary), Josephine (Thomas Irvin Sims), Rebecca (Benjamin Harper), Mariah (Will Dodd), Alice (William Stalmaker), Jasper (unknown), and Newton (Alice Jones). (Courtesy of Berta Dodd.)

**The Ingle-Blanton-Denson-Cowart-Blake House in Double Springs.** Andrew Jackson Ingle built the house above in 1885–1887. When he died in 1896, it was occupied by Circuit Judge R.L. Blanton, then Tom Denson of Fa-So-La fame, and still later by Double Springs businessman Bart Cowart. Dr. Thomas M. Blake bought the property in 1910 and his son, Malcolm Blake, was born there. Years later, Malcolm sold the property to the county. Winston County historian Wynelle Dodd tried to save the structure but had little public support. Finally, as Wynelle wrote in the *Double Springs Scrapbook*, "in the name of progress, this beautiful historic old home was demolished in 1982." Ironically, it was destroyed to make room for a new jail that was never built. Fortunately, artist Tom Sangster preserved its memory with the above sketch. (Courtesy of Don Dodd and Tom Sangster, *Alabama Hill Sketches*.)

**HANCOCK COUNTY'S ONLY SHERIFF.** Pictured are Jane (Collins) Ferris and Willis Ferris (1814–1888) of Larissa. Hancock County's first and only sheriff, Willis served from 1850 to 1859 through the name change to "Winston" in 1858. He was reelected as Winston County sheriff in 1859 and, except for a Civil War term of William Curtis, served until succeeded by First Alabama Cavalry veteran Jonathan Barton of Black Swamp in 1865. (Courtesy of Gerry and Melissa Farris.)

**REV. CURTIS, PASTOR, EDUCATOR, AND THE FIRST MAYOR OF DOUBLE SPRINGS.** Authur Benton Curtis (1885–1957), son of Jim and Mina Curtis, married Ida Corbin. In 1917, he was appointed superintendent of education and served for eight years. In 1943, he became the first mayor of the newly incorporated town of Double Springs. Curtis pastored churches at Phil Campbell, Meek, Arley, and Grayson. He had three sisters: Della, who died young, and Lucy and Annie, who married Hunter brothers Bert and Herb. (Courtesy of Carolyn Hunter.)

**Bart J. Cowart (1872–1954).** Cowart was born on a farm near Double Springs, married Mary Elizabeth Hilton in 1891, and was a Double Springs merchant and editor of the *Winston Herald* (a name he changed to *The New Era*) for a decade before moving to Nauvoo. After a fire destroyed his Nauvoo store, Bart moved to Haleyville, where he was involved in business and real estate. He served Winston, Blount, and Cullman Counties as a state senator in the early 1930s. (Courtesy of Myrtle Blake Lester.)

**The Judge John Bennett Weaver House in Double Springs.** Built in the 1880s, this home began as a two-room log house with a dog-trot in the middle. A kitchen and bedroom were added. In the 1890s, Bart Cowart owned the house and planted water oaks hauled with a mule and wagon from Rock House Branch. John B. Weaver bought the house from Mr. Prickle, a merchant, in 1904. Three rooms, two fireplaces, and porches were added to the house in 1919. It was occupied until 1968. (Courtesy of Sam Weaver.)

**The Robert Alexander Hill Home.** North of Highway 278 on the east side of Sipsey River sits the ancestral home of the Hill family. Descendants, including the F.O. Burdick family, referred to this home as the "Camp," perhaps because Camp Riverside (a 1930s CCC camp) was located here. Bettye Steele Watters, who was born in the Hill house, said it was built in 1902. (Courtesy of Sallie Cox.)

**Dr. William E. and Nancy Howell's Home on Twentieth Street.** Dr. Howell's vineyard and office was to the west of his home, toward the railroad. The Haleyville Public Library in the center of downtown is now on this site, which earlier was the location of the post office. (Courtesy of Margeurite Welborn through BF/NWA.)

**The Haley Home on the Hill.** Walker W. Haley's home, built in Haleyville in 1908, burned in 1971. The site is presently home to Bill's Dollar Store (Sparko). (Courtesy of BF/NWA.)

**The John Dodd House.** This home was built in Haleyville in 1910. John Dodd gave it to his youngest daughter, Alta, upon her marriage to Whit Sparks. In 1989, State Farm Insurance was housed here. It is located between the current *Northwest Alabamian* newspaper office and the Cowart-Faulkner store. (Courtesy of BF/NWA.)

**The "Singing" Speer Family of Houston.** Locally well-known gospel singers, the Speer family includes the following, from left to right: (front row): Mary and Pearl; (second row) Emma (with her doll and her dad), Harry (the baby held by his mother), Tom, Bell, and Ira; (back row) Sam (with a fiddle), father Jim, Dick, and mother Mary. (Courtesy of Donna Wilson Gunnin.)

**Pat Buttram and Maxwell Chapel.** Pat's father, "Mac" Buttram, entered the Methodist ministry licensed from the Maxwell Chapel Methodist Church in 1912, a church his parents organized. His first assignment was Addison, where Pat was born in 1915. Pat was named Maxwell Emmet Buttram for his mother's family, the Maxwells. He always loved Winston County and briefly retired to Camp Maxwell for three months in 1980. (Courtesy of Gus Buttram.)

**MAXWELL EMMETT "PAT" BUTTRAM (1915–1994).** Pat is Winston County's best-known actor, sidekick to Gene Autry and the famous "Mr. Haney" on the series *Green Acres*. His parents were Wilson McDaniel "Mac" Buttram and Mary Emmett (Maxwell) Buttram. Pat had three brothers—Gus, a Methodist minister, who owns and runs Camp Maxwell with wife, Rebecca (Epps) Buttram; Robert Corry; and Johnny—and one sister, Peggy. He died in California in 1994 and was returned to Maxwell Chapel. (Courtesy of Gus Buttram.)

**PAT BUTTRAM (1915–1994), FROM "WINSTON COUNTY FLASH" TO *GREEN ACRE'S* "MR. HANEY."** Pat performed as the "Winston County Flash" with the National Barn Dance program before he met Gene Autry. He was nominated for an Oscar for his role in Alfred Hitchcock's *The Jar*. He then used his well-recognizable deep voice in a number of Walt Disney animated cartoons before landing the "Mr. Haney" role opposite Eddie Albert and Eva Gabor. (Courtesy of Gus Buttram.)

**RUTH JOHNSON, JUDGE FRANK M. JOHNSON, AND THEIR DOBERMAN, NEBUCHADNESSAR.** Judge Johnson loved fishing and golf and was often accompanied by his lifelong friend, U.S. Deputy Marshal "Pert" Dodd. Frank, of Haleyville, was said to have been sent by his father to military school, partially to get him away from "rowdy companions" in Double Springs, including Dodd and Frank Wilson. His Winston County individualistic and character-building background served him well as a federal judge trying to objectively follow the Constitution and the rule of law in South Alabama during the turbulent 1950s and 1960s. His fairness, firmness, and reasoned judgements are legendary. (Courtesy of Ruth Johnson.)

**Judge and Mrs. Frank Minis Johnson in Their Living Room in Montgomery.** The bonnet top highboy chest at the far left was built by Judge Johnson. As a trial judge in Montgomery for 24 years, this Winston County native called up all the toughness he acquired growing up in the hills to ignore constant threats by the Ku Klux Klan and the like (and occasional bombings) to apply the rule of law to highly emotional issues. He lived a quote from Lincoln: "I'll do the very best I know how—the very best I can; and I mean to keep doing so until the end. If the end brings me out all right, what is said against me won't amount to anything. If the end brings me our wrong, ten angels swearing I was right would make no difference." In the end his most severe critics, such as Gov. George Wallace and the Alabama Legislature, admitted they were wrong and Judge Johnson was right. (Courtesy of Ruth Johnson.)

**Judge Johnson Honored in His Hometown of Haleyville, July 1995.** Pictured at the unveiling of a historical marker in front of the Haleyville City Hall dedicated to "The Honorable Frank Minis Johnson, Jr." are, from left to right, Mayor Larry Gilliland, Judge Johnson, and Mrs. Frank (Ruth) Johnson. Ruth's sister, Jewell Norris of Haleyville, is seated in the front center (with her head turned). (Courtesy of Ruth Johnson.)

**U.S. District Judge Ira DeMent, "Winston County Republican."** Ira DeMent, the district judge for the Middle District of Alabama, was appointed a federal district judge in 1992. Judge DeMent spent many of his summers with his grandparents in Double Springs. His grandfather was a justice of the peace who once fined future judge Frank M. Johnson $5 for fighting. His grandmother ran a boardinghouse across the road from Hilton's Gin and Sawmill. (Courtesy of Judge Ira DeMent.)

**THE DRAKE-ADERHOLT HOUSE IN HALEYVILLE, C. 1910.** R.L. Blanton built this house in 1910. Burris Hartwell Drake bought it about 1917 and O.P. and Ada Drake grew up here. Clyde Putnam remodeled it in the 1990s and sold it to Robert and Caroline (McDonald) Aderholt. It is now the Haleyville residence of Congressman and Mrs. Aderholt, their daughter, Mary Elliott, and two cats, O.P. and Miss Ada. (Courtesy of Amy Bartlett-Dodd.)

**CONGRESSMAN ROBERT ADERHOLT, HIS WIFE, CAROLINE McDONALD ADERHOLT, AND THEIR DAUGHTER, MARY ELLIOTT, ON THE STEPS OF THE CAPITOL IN WASHINGTON D.C., 1999.** Congressman Aderholt was re-elected in 1998 to his second term representing the Fourth Congressional District of Alabama. He attended public schools in Haleyville, college at Birmingham Southern, and graduated from the Cumberland School of Law at Samford University. He served as legal assistant to Gov. Fob James and as a municipal judge in Haleyville before being elected to Congress in 1996. In Congress, he serves on the Appropriations Committee and their subcommittees on Transportation and Infrastructure and the District of Columbia. He has supported Social Security, home health care benefits, Alabama transportation projects, the protection of steelworkers jobs from foreign competition, budgeting to reduce the national debt and find tax breaks for families and small businesses and the display of the Ten Commandments in public places. (Courtesy of Congressman Robert Aderholt.)

*Six*

# Country Stores and Smalltown Businesses

**Fred Burdick and D.N. Hall at the Historic Pan-Am, Double Springs.** Built in 1939–40, the Pan-Am Café, Service Station, and Greyhound Bus Station near the old WCHS, saw soldiers off to war, fed hundreds of school kids, and gave many a 25¢ Greyhound ride home. Owners through the years included Verlon Amick, Sylvia Amick, Tom Overton, Ervin Hampton, Opal Smith, Ralph and Myrtle Lester, Sid Ricketts, Frances Lee, and Dallas Overton. (Courtesy of Josh Robinson.)

**A 1902 ADDISON STORE.** Pictured in front of a store in the Addison community are, from left to right, Lillian Steele, George Washington Steele (son of Arzula and John Wesley Steele), John Irvin "Buddy," Alice Orton Steele, Arzula Samples Steele, Mamie Steele, Grandmother Orton, Grandfather Dave Orton, Mae Orton, Minnie Orton, Lillian Orton, "Uncle Doc" Orton, unknown, and Jim Orton. (Courtesy of George David Steele.)

**EDMONDS' GROCERY AND TAVERN, C. 1890S.** J.E. Edmonds' grocery store, which also contained a saloon, was located at Natural Bridge. The wooden building later burned. (Courtesy of Floyd Downey through Bettye Steele Watters and *NWA*.)

**Haley Brothers' Store in Haleyville (1899).** Charles L. Haley (far left) is perched on a New Home Sewing Machine as clerk M. S. Drewry (far right) shows a customer a bolt of calico. Standing in the aisle (third from right) looking on is Walker W. Haley. The Haleys were born at Buttachatchee in Marion County and moved to Davis Cross Roads to establish a business on the Northern Alabama Railroad. (Courtesy of BF/NWA.)

**The Alford-Martin Store, 1906–1907.** The sketch above shows the picturesque Houston landmark built by Bob Stewart for Will Everett. Will Rowe bought it from Everett who sold it to Marshall Alford in 1937. Alford operated the store until the early 1970s. Tommy Martin built a store across the street and used the old store for storage. Tom Sangster sketched the store in 1980. (Courtesy of Don Dodd and Tom Sangster, *Alabama Hill Sketches*.)

**Hiller's Store at Arley.** A number of folks are gathered for this photograph of the "Old Claude Hiller" store. Third from the right is Samuel Hiller, who lost his right leg fighting for the Confederacy in the Civil War. The Hiller house is on the left, behind the store. (Courtesy of Stella Woodard Pratt.)

**The Drewrey Brothers' Mercantile Store in Haleyville, 1907–1920.** Located on the corner of Twentieth Street and Ninth Avenue, Drewrey Brothers' sold general merchandise, furniture, and coffins. (Courtesy of Clara Drewrey Mille through *NWA*.)

**The Shipman Brothers' Store in Haleyville, early 1900s.** When this two-story frame building burned, it was replaced in 1911 by the brick building below. N.W. Freeman was postmaster, and in this pre-1911 photo, the two carriers are Elmer Shipman and John Carey (the first rural mail carrier in Haleyville). (Courtesy of Elmer Shipman through BF/*NWA*.)

**Feldman's Department Store in Haleyville, since 1914.** David Feldman's Department Store was build by John Dodd in 1911 and operated as a hardware and dry good store. David Feldman was the son of Moses Feldman, born in Latvia in 1887, and the daughter of Fannie Royal Feldman of Poland. (Courtesy of Kin Dodd and *NWA*.)

**The Home Front in the "European War."** This July 4, 1917 celebration at the Haleyville "square" features the Traders and Farmers Bank on the right and Feldman's, The Racket Store, and McConnell's Department Store on the left. The U.S. entered World War I the next spring, in April 1918. (Courtesy of Jack Lakeman through BF/*NWA*.)

**Foster's Drugstore on Twentieth Street, Haleyville, 1919.** Pictured in front of Foster's Drugstore, from left to right, are C.E. Miller, Dr. William E. Howell, owners Earlene and Henry Foster with their son, Henry Howell Foster, and an unknown person on the sidewalk bench. (Courtesy of Marguerite Welborn through BF/*NWA*.)

**THE COWART MOTOR COMPANY IN HALEYVILLE, 1919–1928.** Bart Cowart was a merchant in Double Springs and Nauvoo before moving to Haleyville. He built a brick building near the Cleere Hotel to house his new Ford dealership. In 1924, Bart sold 420 Fords at $389.30 each. He subsequently ran Cowart's Music and Jewelry Shop, served as state senator, and engaged in commercial construction, including the Firestone Building operated by his son Lacy. (Courtesy of Luther Tittle through BF/NWA.)

**SAM "LESTER" VANN'S PRESS SHOP IN HALEYVILLE, 1923.** Located in the former office of Dr. W.E. Howell, Sam's third pressing ship sported a "Press While U Wait" sign on the building's corner. The first shop helped pay Sam's tuition at the Methodist Northwest High School. He later worked for the post office while his wife ran the business with their son Sam. (Courtesy of BF/NWA.)

**THE COWART-FAULKNER STORE, 1937.** As the etching on the storefront proclaims, B.J. Cowart built this store in 1937, the year Haleyville High School opened next door. When the high school moved to its new complex in 1964, the junior high, and then the 21st Street Elementary students, occupied the building. Tom Sangster sketched the store in 1980. (Courtesy of Don Dodd and Tom Sangster, *Alabama Hill Sketches*.)

**THE DOUBLE SPRINGS FORD DEALERSHIP, 1926.** Double Springs was a busy place of commerce in 1926, as shown in this photo of the old Ford service station and car dealership owned by Arthur McDonald (far left) and his partner, Ollie Hunter (second from left). Also pictured are Essery Smith, Burt Hunter, Reece Clark, and Al Cole. This building later became Travis Crittenden's Furniture Store, the Otasco store, and is now owned by Debbie Bonds. (Courtesy of Darryal Jackson.)

**"Hughes City" Service Station, 1928.** Hugh Albright owned this business near Rocky Ravine City Park in Haleyville. W.L. Hughes had rental houses across the street and called the area "Hughes City." An ad read: "Come to Hughes City and enjoy our park, bring your children and let them swing and slide, bring your grandmother and let her dance, bring your husband and let him preach. Then if you appreciate this park and playground, buy your gas and oil at Hughes City." (Courtesy of Luther Tittle through BF/NWA.)

**Haleyville Newspapers in the early 1900s.** Pictured above is the newspaper office of the Haleyville *Spotlight* in the 1930s. Earlier newspapers included the *Haleysville Enterprise* (1903), *The Square Deal* (1906), *The Winston County Times* (1906), and the *Haleyville Advertiser* (1922 and *Advertiser Journal*, 1924–1935). (Courtesy of BF/NWA.)

**DORTHEN WADSWORTH'S STORE AT ARLEY, 1930S.** Dorthen, the son of Jesse E. and Dessa Lindley Wadsworth, started working in the family store in 1936 and, except for a World War II stint, 1942–1946, has been there since. He and his wife, Ilene McCurley, have been the sole proprietors since 1962. Both Jess and Dorthen served on the county boards of commissioners/revenue and were primary benefactors of Meek High School . . . Jesse getting the high school there and Dorthen keeping it in Arley by securing three bridges through Gov. John Patterson to avoid isolation after the building of Smith Lake. Jesse's father, Thomas Wadsworth, was the first postmaster at Dismal, serving 1891 to his death in 1897. Both Thomas and his brother John (son of Dr. William and Lula Jack Wadsworth of Oneonta) served in Co. D, 12th Cavalry Tennessee, so the Wadsworths were Republicans with Union Army roots like so many other hill county families. Dorthern and Ilene have one daughter, Sheila, who married Frank Guthrie, and three grandchildren—Devin, Tanya, and Brett. (Courtesy of Don Dodd and Tom Sangster, *Alabama Hill Sketches*.)

**RAY MOTOR COMPANY, HALEYVILLE'S CHEVROLET DEALERSHIP.** Employees admire the new 1932 Chevrolet. From left to right are H.E. "Pete" Ray, Floyd McNutt, Clyde Howell, W.A. Ray, Guy Ray, Silas Hunt, Whitt Evans, and Jimmy Gentle. Employees not shown include bookkeeper Mae Tedder (Mrs. Pete Ray) and mechanics Charlie Cummens and Stanley Williams. From 1933 to 1981, Ray Motor Co. was run by Guy and Pete Ray, sons of W.A. Ray. (Courtesy of Mae Ray through BF/NWA.)

**MARTIN'S WOCO PEP GAS STATION IN DOUBLE SPRINGS.** Newlyweds Vernon and Virnie Martin opened this Woco Pep service station across the street from the courthouse in June 1950. John McVay, and later Ed Snoddy, had a title-search/abstract office behind the station. (Courtesy of Mrs. L.V. Martin.)

**LYNN, AL, IN SOUTHWEST WINSTON COUNTY, 1952.** The first pavement was laid on Lynn streets in 1952, the same year Lynn incorporated as a city. Standing, from left to right, are Vaudrie Tittle, Rex Lindler, and John Pendley. Benny Barton's Barber Shop was located between the post office on the left and John T. Harris' store at the end of the block. (Courtesy of Kin Dodd and *NWA*.)

**A LUMBER CAMP COMMUNITY IN BANKHEAD NATIONAL FOREST, GRAYSON, AL.** Clancy Lumber Company's company town, once with commissary, movie theatre, and post office, became Grayson, AL. The Church of the Forest is nearby, just off Highway 33. (Courtesy of Amy Bartlett-Dodd.)

*Seven*

# Churches, Hospitals, Hotels, and Schools

**Haleyville High School, 1908.** Haleyville High School cost $15,000. The first principal was J.M. Crowell, who was paid a salary of $990. H.G. Dowling became the principal in 1911 after being a school administrator in Dora, Jasper, and Montevallo. The faculty members, all unmarried women, included Ada Drake, Ethel Farrington, Elizabeth Hodges, Kate Howard, and Jennie Jones. Teacher's salaries averaged $415. (Courtesy of BF/NWA.)

**THE CLEERE HOTEL, EARLY 1900S.** W.H. and Mattie Cleere came to Haleyville about 1898 and bought land from W.S. Biddle in 1900 to built the first Cleere Hotel. The two-story wooden structure above burned in 1916–1917. As was often the case, it was replaced by a two-story brick structure. Before the popular use of the automobile, it mainly served railroad passengers, especially traveling salesmen or "drummers" who drummed up business from Haleyville merchants. (Courtesy of BF/NWA.)

**THE SECOND CLEERE HOTEL, 1917.** The Cleere was a popular hotel known for hospitality and outstanding food. Mattie, a gracious host, was assisted by two employees, "Uncle Albert," who transported guests in a horse-drawn bus, and "Uncle George," considered the best cook in northwest Alabama. Room and board cost $2. Individual meals were 50¢. Before the building was torn down in the 1980s, it was operated as a nursing home. (Courtesy of BF/NWA.)

**The First Baptist Church of Haleyville, 1902.** Built on the corner of Ward Alley and Ninth Avenue in 1902, the First Baptist Church was valued at $400. Haleyville Baptists had earlier met in the Church of Christ building located near the Mineral Springs Hotel. Pastors between 1901 and 1910 included Enoch Windes, R.L. Quinn, F.H. Watkins, Thomas P. Sutherland, B.F. Shanks, John A. Huff, and J.T. Johnson. (Courtesy of BF/*NWA*.)

**The First Baptist Church of Haleyville, 1912**. B.H. Drake donated the lot for the church. Plans called for a $10,000 building but the final cost was $16,000. Pastors between the years 1913 and 1987 were John Cunningham, John Huff, C.N. James, L.L. Heam, V.C. Kincaid, J.W. Rucker, W.T Mims, Walter G. Nunn, Harvey C. Love, T.B Stringfellow, and Richard Trader. (Courtesy of BF/*NWA*.)

**The Mineral Springs Hotel and Club House, 1907–1908.** The Mineral Springs Hotel was built across the hollow from the Homestead Restaurant of recent years to serve folks who came to drink the mineral water and to provide room and board for the railroad men. An herbal doctor, Benjamin Wallace Roden, practiced nearby. It was operated by Mr. and Mrs. J.C. Carruth as the Carruth Hotel (1920–1940) until Albert Williams bought it for the lumber. (Courtesy of BF/NWA.)

**Dr. William R. Snow's Hospital, Falls City, c. 1910–1919.** Dr. Snow attended Chattanooga Medical School, practiced in Savannah, GA, and returned to Fall City about 1911 to build a hospital. He closed his hospital when the Walker County Hospital was built in 1922 but continued a regular practice until 1961. He served life-long patients after retirement and delivered his last baby at age 90. (Courtesy of Wynelle Shaddix Dodd.)

**Haleyville's Main Street, 1916.** Electric power and water (note the fire hydrant) were available by this time but the street remained unpaved. The Haley building on the left housed the dental offices of Dr. John Robinson and Dr. H.V. Mashburn, the *Haleyville Journal* newspaper, and the City Pressing Shop. Ozah McConnell's Department Store is on the right; short of it is Farley's Stand. (Courtesy of Telia Dobbs through BF/NWA.)

**Haleyville in 1917, Main Street Facing East.** Dixie Theatre is "behind the ladder" now. In 1917, moving right to left, are Mrs. Steele's Restaurant (with the Winston Telephone Co. and Dr. Cofield's dental office in the building), W.F. Fuller and Son's Grocery, Foster's Drug Store, and Dr. W.E. Howell's office and home. (Courtesy of Marguerite Welborn through BF/NWA.)

**A 1927 Aerial View of Haleyville.** Mrs. Billie Fortenberry identified the buildings in this aerial with the assistance of Mrs. Louise Fields. In many cases it was known that certain businesses were in Haleyville in 1927 but their specific locations had been lost with the passage of time. Due to her exhaustive work with Haleyville newspapers, Billie is one of the few people who could identify Haleyville businesses this well. (Courtesy of BF/NWA.)

## Buildings on the Left

Garrison's house
(behind Feldman's)
Feldman's Store
The *Haleyville Advertiser Journal*
Cowart and Corbin Mercantile Co.
Israel's Barber Shop
The O. McConnell Store (Lyon's)
The W.E. Suggs and Son Feed Store
The Plaxaco Drug Co.
Willie Doss Dry Goods
W.T. Fullers Grocery
The Winston Hotel (Drewry Building)
The Davis Milling Co.
(behind hotel)
Webb-Owens Hardware Store
J.H. Gentles Store
("Great is the Power of Cash")
The post office
Johnson's Telephone Co.

## Byler Road/Ward Alley

M.G. Thrasher's Blacksmith Shop
(later sold to O. J. Whitworth)
Haley Brothers Mule Barn
Haley's Office Building

## Across Railroad Track

The Cowart Motor Company
The C.M. and J.N. Barber Store
The John Dodd Wholesale Company
Haleyville Feed Store (W.C. Herring)
The J.J. Reece Store

## Other Stores, Location Unknown

Fuller Brothers Market (Ed and Grady)
K.B. McConnell's Cash Store
The D. Bonds Store
The T.J. McClellan Shoe Repair Shop

## Buildings on the Right

(not in order)
Bargarey and Meroney Market
F.M. Bates Grocery
First National Bank
The Style Shoppe, Mae Willis
People's Drug Store
Posey Brothers
("Gifts that Last")
Tennessee Valley Bank
Traders and Farmers Bank
Cleere's Pressing Shop
G.W. Bennett's Furniture Store
Bates and Tullis Barber Shop
Vann's Cleaners
(behind Bates and Tullis)
Walker Hardware Store
Holbert House
(behind Hardware Store)
The L.C. Fuller Grocery Store
The Alabama Power Company
Powell's Bakery
J.B. Fuller Grocery
(his first store in town)
Foster's Drug Store
Dr. W.E. Howell's Office
Dr. W.E. Howell's House
Ray Motor Company
Willis Furniture

**HALEYVILLE, 1920s.** Haleyville's Main Street is lined with Henry Ford's Model-Ts in this early 1920s shot looking east from the Traders and Farmers Bank corner (on the right). (Courtesy of Telia Dobbs through BF/*NWA*.)

**HALEYVILLE FIREFIGHTERS IN THE 1920s.** S.L. Vann poses on the fender as a tall and lanky Tim Walker stands on the running board in this photo of Haleyville's firefighters. Will Walker, in the dark vest, is behind Tim's left shoulder. Others include Ozah McConnell, L.C. Fuller, Bob Jackson, R. Tullis, Henry Foster, Jasper Tingle, Whit Sparks, G. McRed, E. Israel, and George King. (Courtesy of Earl Frank Walker through BF/*NWA*.)

**The Winston County Courthouse at Double Springs, 1927.** The county seat moved from Houston to Double Springs in 1884 when a two-story wooden courthouse was completed. It burned, with all its records, in 1891. Part of the present stone courthouse was completed by Andrew Jackson Ingle and Francis L. Hadder in 1894. An annex was added in 1911 and a fireproof wing and jail in 1919–1930 after the above photo was taken. (Courtesy of U.S. Forest Service.)

**An Double Springs Baseball Team in front of the Tennessee Valley Bank in the early 1900s.** Tom Speer and Jeff Tingle are on the running board; the others in the automobile are, from left to right, Wirley Welborn, Hence Wade, James Tingle, James Guttery, Dewey Mitchell, Bartley Corbin, and Jim Ellis. (Courtesy of Catherine Bailey through the *Double Springs Scrapbook*.)

**Dr. Thomas Morgan Blake (1872–1935) at His Home, the Ingle House.** Dr. Blake graduated from Nashville Medical College in 1907 and practiced medicine from then until his death in 1935. He and his wife, Docia Vashti Hill (1886–1970), daughter of Robert Alexander Hill and Sarah Margaret (Lane) Hill, lived in the Andrew Jackson Ingle house from 1907 until their deaths. Dr. Blake's two sons, Robert Forney (1913–1970) and Thomas Malcolm (1917–1989), also became physicians. (Courtesy of Myrtle Blake Lester.)

**Dr. Bonds and Family of Double Springs, c. 1921–1922.** Dr. William Riley Bonds Jr. (1863–1945), his wife, Ada Beard Bonds, and Dr. Bond's brother, Alvin W. Bonds (1853–1948) are pictured in Dr. Bonds' front yard with the courthouse in the background. Dr. Bonds came with his family to Double Springs in 1871 from Gwinett County, GA. (Courtesy of Mona Kidd.)

**Dr. Bonds' Office, Double Springs Library, c. 1911.** From 1947 until the building of the community center, this distinctive rock structure, once the office of Dr. William R. Bonds, served as a library. Mrs. Clara McCullar was librarian from 1953 to 1967; later librarians include Maebeth McVay, Emerald Kemp, Pinky Adkins, Ann Page, Ada Godsey, Gloria Sutherland, Hazel Gerrard, Charlotte Shaddix, and Jean Overton. (Courtesy of Don Dodd and Tom Sangster, *Alabama Hill Sketches.*)

**The Snoddy Hospital, Haleyville's First Hospital.** The hospital was operated by Sam and John Snoddy from 1928 until it burned in 1930. The building was the former home of Warner Flack, an ICRR engineer, who purchased it from the builder, F.M. Blanton. Pinkard's Funeral Home is on the site now. (Courtesy of BF/NWA.)

**THE HALEYVILLE CITY "SQUARE," 1941.** On the right is Traders and Farmers' Bank, Dr. Robert Blake's Clinic, Yost's 10¢ Store, Hayes Hardware, and the Alabama Power Company. On the left is Lyon's Department Store, McAfee's Appliance Store (with Hotpoint Appliances), Dobbs Hardware, and Long's Drugstore. (Courtesy of Telia Dobbs through BF/*NWA*.)

**A DOUBLE SPRINGS STREET SCENE FROM THE 1940–1950s.** About the time of this photograph, Winston County had a centennial celebration; several decades later, in 1983, Double Springs had its centennial. This inspired the publication of *Double Springs Scrapbook*, periodic "Free State Festivals," the Dual Destiny Civil War statue, the Looney's Tavern outdoor pageant, and a rekindled awareness of the Free State's unique history and culture. (Courtesy of the *Double Springs Scrapbook*.)

**GEORGE CRANFORD BERRY (1911–1999).** World War II veteran "Crant" Berry grew up "moonshining," but came to be sheriff of Winston County. He "cut down" 455 whiskey stills in his first term and 225 in his second, which he won without a run-off against five other candidates. Deputies James Dodd and W.H. Burns, on the right, behind Crant, are seated on the sidewalk wall in front of the Haleyville City Hall. (Courtesy of Nell, Katrina, and Kottnie Berry.)

**AN EARLY 1950S STILL SEIZURE.** Seated to the left of the still are Raymond Cobb and an unidentified gentleman. Standing, from left to right, are Sheriff Clifford Peak, Deputy Roy Posey, Sam Posey, and Chief Deputy Jasper Bailey. Roy Posey and Raymond Cobb were later sheriffs of Winston County. (Courtesy of Cora Lee Peak Whatley.)

**A 1960 Aerial View of Haleyville.** Mrs. Billie Fortenberry made the following identifications after talking with 14–15 people in early 2000. Part of the difficulty was matching a specific business and building to one year. Also, small businesses change owners often and, of course, memories fade as the years go by. Billie said finding the businesses to match the 1960 buildings was one of the hardest historical jobs she has ever undertaken. Obviously she did it well. (Courtesy of BF/NWA.)

## Left Side of Twentieth Street from Highway 13 (Eleventh Avenue) Looking West

The Pure Oil Service Station
(Wallace Brown)
Dick Williams Taxi
The fire station
(back of the courthouse)
Vann's Dry Cleaners
The Alabama Power Company
The Barcliff Furniture Company
Drake and Driver
The post office
Mitchell's Drug Company
Mildred Barber's Flower Shop
The Dixie Theatre
The Duncan Jewelry Shop
Dependable Service Center
Teague's Electric
Haye's Hardware
Trader's and Farmer's Bank
State National Bank
Marshall Pierce's Pool Room
Norris Berry's Barber Shop
Pace Jewelry
Western Auto
William's Market

## Nineteenth Street Looking West

The Manasco-Maneval Hospital
The Presbyterian Church (inactive)
Presbyterian Manse
(Walter Miller lived there)
Haleyville Laundry and Cleaners
Shipman's Dry Cleaners
Holdbrook's Boarding House
(formerly Meroney's)
*The Haleyville Advertiser*
(Ninth Avenue)
Haleyville Machine and Welding Shop
Barber's Wholesale Grocery
Baker's Furniture
The Cockrell-West Motor Company

## Right Side of Twentieth Street Looking West

Horn's Men Store
Cowart's Firestone Home
and Auto Store
The Reece Appliance Company
The McNutt Service Station
McGuire's Electric and Plumbing
Green's Fabrics
The Blue Ribbon Café
Top's Furniture
G.W. Gaskin and Son Grocery
The Harris Drug Store
Dobb's Furniture
Field's Cotton Bowl
Odum's
Sherman's
Elliott's Shoe Store
Burleson's Men Store
Lou-Rays's
Dobb's Hardware
V.J. Elmore's 5 and 10 cent Store
King's
Whitt's Jewelry Store
Velma's
Lyon's Department Store
Israel's Barber Shop
Mauldin's
Feldman's

## Tenth Avenue

Long's Grocery
Ray Motor Company and Body Shop

## Ward Alley/Byler Road

Wakefield's Radio Shop
Luke's Second Hand Store
Professional Building
The Drewry Building
Cagle's Café
Whitworth's Blacksmith Shop

**Dr. Malcolm Blake's Memorial Monument, Double Springs.** Without living in Double Springs during the nearly half-century Dr. Blake was everyone's family doctor, one cannot comprehend the esteem to which he was held. As Tom Bartlett wrote on the marble tribute next to his unpretentious office, he was "the perfect model for the legendary country doctor." Without doubt, he was the most beloved public figure in the history of Double Springs. Malcolm and wife, Jayne, had one daughter, Frances Ann. (Courtesy of Amy Bartlett-Dodd.)

**Winston Physicians.** In 1976, there were five medical doctors living and working in Winston County, all of them native physicians for a number of years. From left to right are John E. Wood, W.K. Wilson, Malcolm Blake, Hobson Manasco, and Ben Moore. With them, at far right, is Burdick-West Hospital Administrator Tillman Hill. (Courtesy off *NWA* and Darryal Jackson.)

**Winston County High School, 1908.** With the election of Braxton Bragg in 1907, a high school was built in each county. WCHS in Double Springs was built of native sandstone. It had a library, laboratory, and large auditorium. C.D. Wade was principal from 1908 to 1910, and B.B. McLeran was made principal in 1911. Teachers in 1911 were W.C. Shotts, Martha DuBose, and Lillie B. Parkman. Tom Sangster did the above sketch from several faded photographs. (Courtesy of *Double Springs Scrapbook*.)

**Winston County High School, Double Springs, 1937–1971.** Built in 1926 and enlarged to include the elementary school in 1939, the building above was consumed by fire in 1971. The native sandstone school matched the courthouse, library, and other town structures that said "Double Springs." Hundreds of students spent their entire public school life in this building. Others transferred here for their last six years. The old rock school, sketched by Tom Sangster from a 1957 photo, was a special place. (Courtesy of *Double Springs Scrapbook*.)

**The Graduating Class of Haleyville High School, 1910.** Pictured from left to right are Ada Drake, Effie Drake, Julia Howell, and Daisey Crowell with Principal J.M. Crowell. The 1911 class included Grady Bates, Willie Biddle, Glenn Biddle, Guy Drake, Kathleen Halbert, Earle Howell, Judge Howell, Willie Lakeman, Mabell Lakeman, Clifford Mayhall, Ollie Miller, Erlene Miller, Berte Montgomery, and Ida Nash. Normal graduates had four years of English, three years of history, three years of science, four years of math, and two years of foreign language. (Courtesy of BF/*NWA*.)

**The Winston County Senior Class, 1925.** Shown here are the following, from left to right: (front row) Egbert Baughn, Troy Lyle, Shaffer Stanford, Sylvester Stephens, and Elbert Kidd; (second row) Daisy Alford, Violet Bradfield, Gladys Vaughn, Myrtle Chambers, Velma Blake, Dura Hunter, Mildred Boteler, Lawley Ingle, Leola Looney, Lorus Briscoe, and Floy Ivey; (third row) Agnus Smyle (teacher), Belle Wilson, Madge Howell, Ethel Cockrell, Carrie Seymour, and Grace Bradfield Jacobs; (fourth row) Isadore Burdick, Jess Whatley, W.P. Picklesimer (principal), Otto Smith, and Leonard Mize. (Courtesy of Lorus Briscoe Baggett.)

**HALEYVILLE MUSICIANS, 1917.** Gathered in front of Traders and Farmers Bank are the group of citizens comprising the Haleyville Concert Band. As it was also "Woodsmen of the World" initiation time, a group of new members posed with the band. Included in those pictured are Floyd McNutt, Hugh Stephenson, Theo Jackson, Eslie Owens, Clyde McConnell, Reubin Drewery, James Walker, Buddy Jackson, Luther Tittle, Arlon Bennett, Vernon Martin, Charlie Miller, Will Hulsey, Red Houston Long, Cullen Donaldson, Charlie Maples, Clarence Miller, Pinkney Riddle, Alden Southern, John Posey Sr., Will Blackwell, Walter Brown, Bill Parson, W.E. Christopher, Ebb Wilson, Doc Bonds, Dave Sutherland, Joe Carey, Dr. Sam Snoddy, C.H. Goddard, Sheriff Hunter, Dr. W.E. Howell, V.H. Albright, Jim Riddle, Jack Still, Lawton Reece, Jim Knight, Luther Drake, Homer Bearden, and Bill Ellenburg. (Courtesy of L.C. Tittle and the *NWA*.)

**The Undefeated 1932 Haleyville High School Football Team.** Shown in front of the old Northwest High School is the team that outscored their opposition 367-18. Seven of their nine opponents didn't score (Bear Creek, Hanceville, Lynn, Russelville, Hackleburg, Brilliant, and Vina). They beat Russelville 101-0. Their only close games were at St. Bernard (13-6) and Tuscumbia (27-12). From left to right, they are as follows: (first row) Frank Martin, Herman Martin, Carl Melson, Leo Hicks, Truman Lovett, Elwyn Dobbs, and Ellis Hall; (second row) Gober Howell, Cecil "Buck" Long, Frank Putnam, Earnest "Bear" Smith, Hollis Garrard, James Walker, and William Hugh Clark; (back row) Gervis Doss, Ralph Haynes, Elmer League, Ray Batchelor, Bernard Albright, Bill Hargett, Thomas A. Stevenson, and manager Boots Lovell. (Courtesy of BF/NWA.)

**Winston County High School Teachers in the early 1940s.** From left to right are the following: (front row) Clora Adkins Christian, Ethel Curtis, Barbara Farris, and ? Williams; (back row) Kate Hilton, Jessie B. Wood, Mitchell Drake, Lila K. Overton, and Nell Robinson. (Courtesy of Darryal Jackson.)

**Double Springs Elementary, Second and Third Grades, 1947.** Bert Hunter was principal when Mary Sutherland (Whitfield) taught this combined class. Some of those pictured are Cindy Steele, Loyce Gilliland, Frankie Chilcoat, Pat Gilbreath, W.T Pearson, R.L Colvett, Jimmy Green, Robert Sutton, Tommy Bartlett, Betty Williams, Lona May Smith, Barbara Hyche, Mildred Ellenburg, I.V. Watts, Grady Batchelor, Parker Lovelady, Kenneth Shaddix, Frank Burdick, Wyatt Lacy Blake, and Darryal Jackson. (Courtesy of Bettye Steele Watters.)

**OLD ADDISON SCHOOL, ADDISON, AL.** This building was the last wooden frame building used by Addison Elementary School. It was torn down and replaced by a brick building in the late 1950s. Addison High School occupied a building of native Winston County sandstone from 1935 to 1992, until being replaced by a new brick building in 1992. (Courtesy of Darryal Jackson.)

**LYNN HIGH SCHOOL, 1967.** Gathered in front of the school are members of the senior class. They are as follows, from left to right: (sitting on left) David Hill, Roger Bell, Allen Cummings, Brenda Wakefield, and Judy Ward; (sitting in middle) Vester Wilemon, Lecil Estill, Hattie Patterson, Ila Mae Priven, Wayne Waldrop, Judy Pike, Gary Harbin, unidentified, and Dwight Ward; (lying down) David Lynn (?); (standing) Dwight Bailey, Bonnie Bailey, Mary Ann Ingle, Delton Cagle, Wayne Edward Guthrie, Letrella Hicks, Linda Noles, Kay Barnett, Terry Farris, Stanley Tittle, Gerry Farris, Melissa Rose, William Willingham, Dennis Tidwell, Delores Myers, and Carol Waldrop. (Courtesy of Gerry and Melissa Rose Farris.)

# *Eight*

# Forest Folk, CCC Camps, and Soldiers

**Pine Torch Church in Bankhead National Forest, c. 1850s.** Pine Torch is one of the oldest log churches in Alabama and was more than a church. Zadoc McVay attended and taught school here. "Uncle Dick" Payne, who named the county "The Free State of Winston," is buried here. Memorial services for Union dead in the Civil War were held here after the war. (Courtesy of Amy Bartlett-Dodd.)

**Elisabeth Jane "Aunt Jenny" Brooks, (1826–1924).** Winston County families viewed a wrong against a family member as something the entire family was obligated to vindicate. No one was better at this than Aunt Jenny Brooks. When her husband, Willis, and son John were killed by Confederate Home Guards, Aunt Jenny made her other children swear to avenge their deaths and brought a son-in-law, Sam Baker, into the feud. For more, see *Sam Baker, Winston County's Gunfighter* (1998). (Courtesy of Edward Herring.)

**The Brooks Boys and Sam Baker, c. 1898.** This photo taken in Paris, TX, shows the following, from left to right: (front) Henry Brooks and Sam Baker; (back) John Brooks, Willis Brooks (father), and Clifton Brooks. (Courtesy of Edward Herring.)

**Sam Baker, Winston County Gunfighter.** This photo graces the back cover of Edward Herring's book on Sam Baker. Shown are Sam and Francis (Brooks) Baker with their daughter Emma, *c.* 1880. (Courtesy of Edward Herring.)

**The African-American-Creek Hubbard Family of the Kinlock Hubbards.** William Hubbard, a slave of David Hubbard, and his wife, Ginsey (a Creek Indian), had a homestead at Kinlock. In 1884, William, sons Hannibal and Henry, and Lawrence County deputies had a "shoot-out" with Aunt Jenny Brook's sons and son-in-law. Hannibal Hubbard's horse was allegedly stolen by Henry Brooks. The Hubbards moved to the Moulton Valley. Henry Brooks and his brother-in-law, Sam Baker, fled to Texas. (Courtesy of Lamar Marshall.)

**Will R. Riddle (1869–1933) and His Son Odes.** Odes, sitting on his fathers knee in this photo, was accidentally shot and killed by a pistol Will had in a trunk is his bedroom. Will blamed Odes' brother, Lonnie, and threatened to kill him. Neighbors put Lonnie on a train to Tennessee to live with relatives while armed men stood off Will at the Haleyville Depot. Lonnie returned home one time, to his father's funeral. (Courtesy of Donna Wilson Gunnin.)

**World War I Soldiers from Winston.** Two soldiers from Haleyville, Ed and Leon Fuller, are pictured here in their uniforms. The first five Winston men drafted were McKinley Lovett, Robert Orton, Noble Pearson, Elzie Thomas, and Sam Weems. George Whitehead, for whom Haleyville's American Legion Post is named, was the first fatality of the war from Winston County. Private John Hoggle, who received the Distinguished Service Cross and the French Croix de Guerre, was apparently the most decorated. (Courtesy of BF/NWA.)

**HALEYVILLE WELCOMES WORLD WAR I HEROES.** On November 11, 1919, Haleyville celebrated the first Armistice Day honoring World War I veterans in front of Mose Feldman's store (to the right not in photo). Across the railroad tracks in the background are, from left to right, Barber's Feed Store, Reece's Blacksmith Shop, and the city jail (top visible). (Courtesy of BF/*NWA*.)

**THE DOUBLE SPRINGS CCC CAMP ON SIPSEY RIVER.** The officers of "Camp Riverside," located east of Sipsey River on the Double Springs-Addison road from 1935to 1939, included Ernest Frazier and Joshua Mann of Double Springs. In the 1933–1942 era, more than 2.5 million youth planted 200 million trees, checked soil erosion, built roads and trails, fought forest fires, and built campgrounds. Wages were $30 a month. Besides food, clothing, shelter, and medical care, they received vocational training and remedial education. (Courtesy of Cora Peak Whatley.)

**THE "CAMP RIVERSIDE" CAFETERIA.** The above dining hall looks very orderly with neatly aligned cups and plates. The "Let's Continue to Excel" sign accents the positive atmosphere. Local members of Company 3476 were James Denson and Issac Downs of Arley; Odalee Gilliland, Theodore Hood, and Clyde Rippy of Addison; Leonard Gilbreath, William Guttery, Troy Lovett, and Carl Weaver of Double Springs; John Johnson of Falls City; and Henry Dunlap of Houston. (Courtesy of Hoyett Wolfe and Maxine Wolfe White.)

**A KINLOCK SPRINGS BASEBALL TEAM, COMPANY 1403, HALEYVILLE.** Haleyville men in the "Haleyville Camp" included leaders Guy Bennett, Ray Lovell, and S.A. Posey; assistant leaders Bernard Albright, Woodrow Chilcoat, R.B. Kiker, Kirby Minor, J.M. Parson, J.M. Shipman, Ezra Smith, and Calvin Tanksley; members W.C. Brooks, Lennie L. Burleson, Joel Carey, Henry Dooley, Ralph Drake, J.C. Herron, Russell Howell, L.W. League, Howard C. Lovell, O.B. McCombs, R.L. Pearson, Walter Posey, D.B. Pugh, Melvin Richard, T.H. Stone, Quinton Veal, S.E. Willis, and Earl Wilson. (Courtesy of Cora Peak Whatley.)

**The Haleyville CCC Camp at Kinlock Springs in Bankhead National Forest.** Young men are shown here working in a rock quarry in the forest. Most Winston County workers at Kinlock were from Haleyville and it was often called the "Haleyville Camp." (Courtesy of Cora Peak Whatley.)

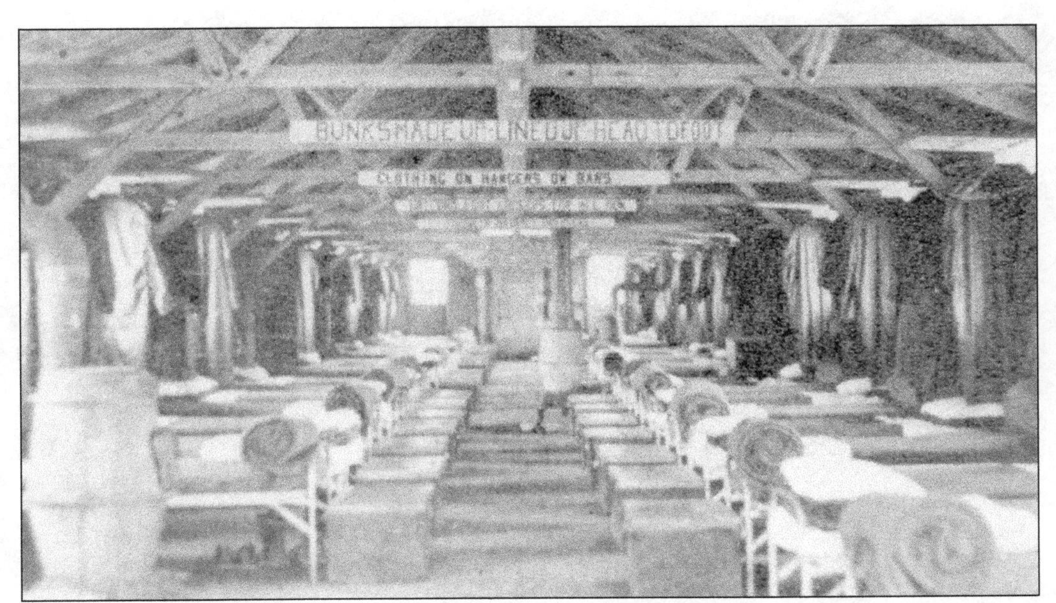

**CCC Camp Barracks.** Pictured is a typical CCC Camp barracks with "Floors fully cleaned and dry," "Bunks made up lined up head to foot," and "Clothing on hangers or bars," signs galore. Probably a bit more regimented than at home. (Courtesy of Cora Peak Whatley.)

**Cadet Fortenberry of Haleyville with His Primary Training Instructor.** Aviation Cadet Ullman Fortenberry is shown in World War II primary training with the PT-17 Stearmen. (Courtesy of Ullman Fortenberry.)

**Lt. Fortenberry and His B-17 Crew in World War II.** First Lt. Ullman J. Fortenberry (top row, far right) of Haleyville stands with his B-17 Flying Fortress crew in the Mediterranean Theater of Operations in World War II. Lt. Fortenberry's crew made two of the longest 15th AF missions of the war. He received a Distinguished Flying Cross for his heroics on the Berlin mission. (Courtesy of Ullman Fortenberry.)

**CORBIN SEYMOUR OF DOUBLE SPRINGS IN WORLD WAR II.** Bartley Corbin Seymour Sr. (1929–1998), son of George and Nettie Corbin Seymour, graduated from WCHS in 1940, served overseas in World War II, and remained in the Army Reserve and National Guard after the war. Although he served for 32 years in the military, Corbin was best known for his 14 years as mayor of Double Springs. (Courtesy of Virginia Seymour.)

**BOBBY DODD OF HALEYVILLE IN THE ARMY AIR CORPS, WORLD WAR II.** Garland Rudolph "Bobby" Dodd was the son of Benjamin and Alta Weaver Dodd. After the war, he ran the Dodd Sales Company of Haleyville, and in the 1960s, an auto parts business at Forkville. A tornado destroyed the Forkville store. It was rebuilt but burned down later. By the 1980s, he and his wife, Charlene, ran a general merchandise business in Haleyville. (Courtesy of Don Dodd.)

**Lt. Junior Grade Ruth Johnson at Miami, 1944.** While Frank M. Johnson of Haleyville fought in France during World War II, his wife, Ruth, served in the Naval Reserve. Ruth was born a "coal miner's daughter" at Carbon Hill in 1919. When the Depression closed the mines in 1929–1930, Ruth's family moved to Haleyville. Finishing high school in 1938, a fond memory was of her and Telia Sue Tubbs (Dobbs) never losing a debating team match. (Courtesy of Ruth Johnson.)

**I.B. Burdick of Double Springs in World War II.** Isadore, shown here in his World War II uniform, returned to Double Springs after a career as an Army officer. He, like brothers Blaine, Burton, and Fred, served Winston County in various county offices, including superintendent of education. I.B. and his wife, Ann, had one child, Frank. (Courtesy of Sallie Cox.)

**The Double Springs Unit of the Alabama National Guard, 1964.** Shown at "Summer Camp" are the following, from left to right: (front row) G.W. Adkins, D. Hendrix, D.W. Moody, D.S. Posey, E.R. Curtis, J.H. Posey, R.D. Jackson, S.L. Weaver, J.E. Green, and G.H. Jones; (second row) E.O. Shipman, E.J. Ayers, K.I. Parrish, P.E. Knowles, H.C. Roberts, P.R. Gilliland, B.R. Tidwell, J.P. Wallace, L.O. Lindley, and B.J. Martin; (third row) F.D. Overton, B.T. Green, R.E. Jackson, D.N. Lawler, D.E. Allcorn, J.Q. Gibson, H.T. Wolfe, S.D. Cole, C.V. Key, and J.T. Wade; (fourth row) E.V. Thompson, W.T. Pearson, K.A. Dooley, B.R. Reynolds, V.L. Pruitt, B.E. Storie, J.D. Curtis, K.E. Overton, H.C. Williamson, and B.H. Lovelady; (fifth row) W.B. Storie, R.E. Baldy, B.J. Dodd, W.L. Williams, D. Farley, M.E. Brewer, R.H. McCombs Jr., B.R. Lovett, J.L. Waid, and J.E. Winkie; (back row) F.R. Williams, E.J. Waid, L.B. Waid, A. Smith, W. McCombs, L.J. Abbott, J.C. Abbott, R.L. Burdick, H.R. Thomas, D.I. Wilson, and W.C. White. (Courtesy of Neal Shipman.)

**DONALD McVAY OF DOUBLE SPRINGS, MARINE VIETNAM VETERAN.** Donald Morgan McVay, son of John and Maebeth (Neely) McVay, graduated from WCHS in 1958 and Florence State in 1962. He married Helen Bonds and joined the Marines in 1963. He won his wings at Pensacola, and a career as a Marine pilot followed, including three tours in Vietnam. He is shown with his favorite aircraft, an OV-10 Bronco. (Courtesy of Donald McVay.)

**INTERNATIONALLY KNOWN NOVELIST, GUS HASFORD (1947–1997).** Between his Haleyville birth and burial at Winston Memorial Gardens, Gus Hasford (the four year old at left) gave a new dimension to Winston County individualism. His first novel was made into the movie *Full Metal Jacket*, a well-received war movie. A conviction for stealing 748 library books may have cost Gus an Oscar. He served in Vietnam, wrote three noteworthy novels, and as a friend noted "got the greatest fine in the history of library science." (Courtesy of Bettye Steele Watters.)

*Nine*

# The Civil War, Going Looney, and Bankhead Forest

THE KINLOCK BLUFF SHELTER, BANKHEAD NATIONAL FOREST. Winston abounds in shelter caves. The Kinlock shelter is one of the largest, and rock art there indicates early Native-American use as a meeting place. They were often used as hideouts from Confederate authorities during the Civil War. The Conscript Bureau estimated "8,000 to 10,000 deserters and Tory conscripts" hiding out in the hills by 1863. (Courtesy of Steven Hicks.)

**The "Dual Destiny" Civil War Statue, Honoring the Soldiers in Both Armies, Double Springs.** The statue by sculptor Branko Medenica has a plaque written by Donald Dodd: "The Civil War was not fought between the North and South but between the Union and Confederate armies. Perhaps as many as 300,000 Southerners served in the Union Army. The majority of the Appalachian South, from West Virginia to Winston County, was pro-Union. Winston County provided 239 Union and 112 Confederate soldiers, 21 of whom shared last names. This Civil War soldier, one-half Union and one-half Confederate, symbolizes the War within a War, and honors the Winstonians in both Armies. Their shiny new swords of 1861 were, by 1865, as broken as the spirits of the men who bore them, and their uniforms of Blue and Gray, once fresh and clean, were now as worn and patched as the bodies and souls they covered. Johnny Reb and Billy Yank, disillusioned by the realities of war, shared Dual Destinies as pragmatic Americans in a reunited nation." (Courtesy of Janet Johnson.)

**The Natural Bridge of Alabama: Winston's Geological Wonder.** "The Bridge" was a landmark of the antebellum and Civil War era and the site of a meeting of 300-400 conscripts, Confederate deserters, and Unionists during the war. As described by John Phillips' diary, they met to decide a course of action. From that meeting, over a hundred men chose to travel together to join the Union Army. (Courtesy of Steven Hicks.)

**FRANK BURDICK, UNION ARMY VETERAN, AND ROBERT ALEXANDER HILL, CONFEDERATE ARMY VETERAN.** Captain Fernando Cortez "Frank" Burdick of New York met two Feltman boys from Fayette County in the First Alabama Cavalry and married their younger sister, Nancy Margaret. Their son, F.O., married Catherine, the daughter of Robert Alexander Hill, a Confederate veteran; therefore, the children of F.O. and Catherine had one grandfather in the Confederate Army and one in the Union Army. (Courtesy of Sallie Cox.)

**JOHN DODD'S FIRST ALABAMA CAVALRY UNION SOLDIER MARKER AT LYNN.** The simple inscription and the slightly curved dome are a common sight in northwest Alabama cemeteries. It represents more than 3,000 white Alabamians who served the United States in the Civil War. In the background (above right) is the grave of John's grandfather, Jesse Dodd, a Revolutionary War veteran. (Courtesy of Janet Johnson.)

**Looney's Tavern Sketch by Bill Tidwell.** Tidwell, a Winston County native and artist, made this sketch based on Elmo Brewer's recollection. Bill Looney guided hundreds to join the Union Army and disposed of his share of Confederates and Home Guards. As bushwhacking continued after the war, the "Black Fox" went west. The famous 1862 neutrality meeting at Looney's inspired the outdoor pageant at Lakeshore on a hill above Smith Lake. (Courtesy of Bill Tidwell.)

**Looney's Board Members at the Ground-breaking, 1989.** Named after the location of the neutrality meeting, and presenting outdoor drama based on the history of the area, the Looney's Tavern complex has become a major tourist attraction. There for the ground-breaking ceremonies were, from left to right, Neal Shipman, Eldon Curtis, Frank Wilson, Blaine Cagle, Dwain Moody, and Wallace Tidwell. (Courtesy of Looney's Tavern Productions.)

**Rev. John Frank Wilson, Looney's Tavern Narrator.** Until recently, Frank Wilson played the folksy, lovable narrator who hobbled back and forth between scenes, integrating them into a smooth-flowing whole with country grace and charm. (Courtesy of Looney's Tavern Production.)

**Looney's Cast in a Montgomery Ballroom Scene during the Secession Convention.** Shown are three major characters in the play. From left to right are "Miss Cherry," played by Elizabeth Ann Wilson, Barry Nichols as "William L. Yancey," and Heath Mahan as "Chris Sheats." (Courtesy of Looney's Tavern Productions.)

**"We Don't Believe in Repeating Gossip."** The Old South cooperative work activity shown in this scene include, from left to right, cast members Debra Williams, Pam Williams, Gail Prueitt, Jennifer Wright, Peggy Denton, and Annis Evans. (Courtesy of Looney's Tavern Productions.)

**Great Costuming!** Local casting in the early days of the drama is illustrated in this ballroom scene. From left to right are Traci Simpson (Russelville), Kristie Rowe Crummie (Gadsden), unidentified, Heath Mahan (Florence), Barry Nichols (Leighton), Timothy Holland (Bear Creek), Beth Wilson (Double Springs), Kelly Wilson (Double Springs), unidentified, David Coston (Florence), Shawn Horton (Arley), Jessica Pulliam (Double Springs), Derek Aaron (Curry), Yvonne Stancel (Cullman), and Deborah Scott (Phil Campbell). At the center, top, are Mary Beth Robinson (Hamilton) and unidentified. (Courtesy of Looney's Tavern Productions.)

**NEAL SHIPMAN, CAPTAIN OF "THE FREE STATE LADY."** Anchored on Smith Lake is a "touring and dining" riverboat operated by Capt. Shipman. Wearing several other hats, he is a "Teller of Tall Tales" and an authentic-looking Santa Claus. One of the original owners of Looney's Tavern, Neal has done it all . . . from playing a preacher in the pageant to extensive public relations work promoting "Going Looney" in the tourist industry. (Courtesy of Looney's Tavern Productions.)

**THE MEN WHO MADE IT HAPPEN.** Looney's Tavern Board of Directors include the following, from left to right: (front row) Eldon Curtis, Blaine Cagle, V.C. Evans, Jimmy Posey, Hoyett Wolfe, and Donald Posey; (back row) Scott Smith, Neal Shipman, John Frank Wilson, Wallace Tidwell, Dwain Moody, Marvin Waid, and Lanney McAlister. (Courtesy of Looney's Tavern Productions.)

**Wallace, in his Favorite Uniform.** Wallace Tidwell, lifetime logger, Looney's Tavern co-founder, preservationist, conservationist, and innkeeper, rents the log cabin he built next to his home to Looney's visitors. (Courtesy of Lamar Marshall.)

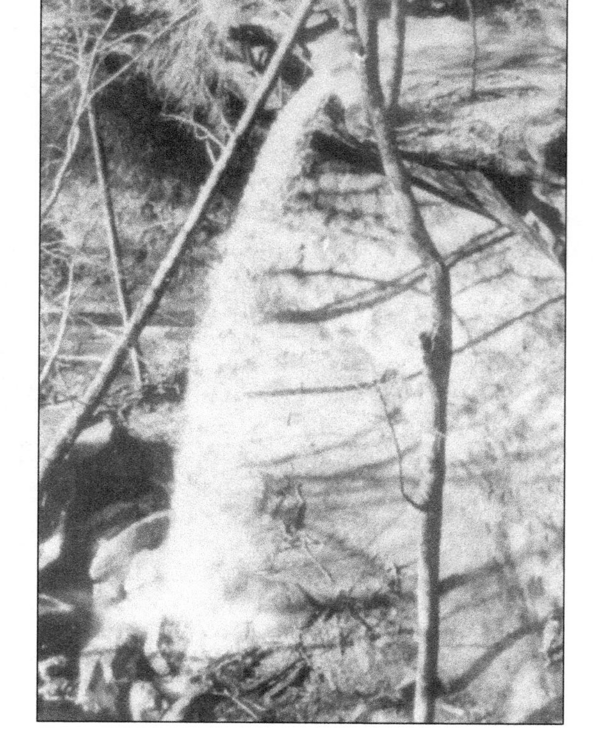

**Bee Branch Falls in the Sipsey Wilderness.** Bee Branch Falls at the big poplar tree in the Bankhead Forest Wilderness Area is one of several waterfalls in this especially scenic area. There are perhaps 100 waterfalls in Bankhead. (Courtesy of Lamar Marshall.)

**MAKING A BASKET, PRESERVING A CULTURE.** Lamar Marshall, publisher of *Wild Alabama* and owner of Wild Alabama Trading Post at Wren, is a "good old boy" turned conservationist. (Courtesy of Lamar Marshall.)

**A MODERN MOUNTAIN MAN OF BANKHEAD.** Jim Manasco, artist and writer, folklorist, Bankhead botanist and guide, and country philosopher, has spent a lifetime promoting Bankhead Forest, constantly interpreting and reinterpreting its history and legends. (Courtesy of Lamar Marshall.)

**THE CAMP MAXWELL WATERFALL, PEBBLE COMMUNITY AT CAMP MAXWELL.** The 70-foot waterfall pictured here is located off the Haleyville-Double Springs highway at Forkville. Camp Maxwell is a Christian youth campground organized in 1946 and still operated by Rev. Gus Buttram and his wife, Rebecca. (Courtesy of Lamar Marshall.)

**THE CHURCH OF THE FOREST, GRAYSON.** Pictured is a church just off the Double Springs-Moulton highway in the Hepsidam-Pine Torch part of Bankhead National Forest. The church was organized by Rev. Arthur B. Curtis in 1946 and built with assistance from the Clancy Lumber Company. Gilbert Burt, M.M. Preston, and James Curry were subsequent pastors. Initial members included the Miles, Bray, and Fitzgerald families. (Courtesy of Amy Bartlett-Dodd.)

**LITTLE UGLY CANYON FALLS.** These falls can be found north of Wolf Pen Cemetery and, like the Soagahoagdee and Caney Creek Falls (which follow), they are located in Bankhead Forest. In 1942, the William B. Bankhead National Forest was named for FDR's speaker of the house (Tallulah's father). It had earlier been known as the Black Warrior National Forest (1936–1942) and the Alabama National Forest (1918–1936). (Courtesy of Lamar Marshall.)

**SOAGAHOAGDEE FALLS OFF BRUSHY CREEK.** (Courtesy of Lamar Marshall.)

**Caney Creek Falls.** (Courtesy of Lamar Marshall.)

Printed in the USA
CPSIA information can be obtained
at www.ICGtesting.com
LVHW081958120923
757853LV00009B/599